# Crisis in Intimacy

# Crisis in Intimacy

**Jacquelyn B. Carr**
*Foothill College*

*Brooks/Cole Publishing Company*
*Pacific Grove, California*

**Brooks/Cole Publishing Company,** *A Division of Wadsworth, Inc.*

© 1988 by Wadsworth, Inc., Belmont, California 94002. All rights reserved.
No part of this book may be reproduced, stored in a retrieval system, or
transcribed, in any form or by any means—electronic, mechanical,
photocopying, recording, or otherwise—without the prior written permission
of the publisher, Brooks/Cole Publishing Company, Pacific Grove, California
93950, a division of Wadsworth, Inc.

Printed in the United States of America
10  9  8  7  6  5  4  3  2  1

*Library of Congress Cataloging-in-Publication Data*

Carr, Jacquelyn B., [date]-
  Crisis in intimacy / Jacquelyn B. Carr.
    p.    cm.
  Bibliography: p.
  Includes index.
  ISBN 0-534-09006-0 (pbk.) :
  1. Interpersonal relations.  2. Intimacy (Psychology)    I. Title.
HM132.C355 1988
158'.2—dc19                              87-32560
                                              CIP

Sponsoring Editor: *Claire Verduin*
Editorial Associate: *Linda Ruth Wright*
Production Editor: *Phyllis Larimore*
Manuscript Editor: *Robert Fiske*
Permissions Editor: *Carline Haga*
Interior and Cover Design: *Lisa Thompson*
Typesetting: *Kachina Typesetting, Inc., Tempe, Arizona*
Printing and Binding: *Diversified Printing & Publishing Services, Inc.,*
                          *Brea, California*

# Preface

L ife is inherently full of paradox, ambiguity, and incon-
sistency. This rich confusion of the human condition cou-
pled with our freedom to choose often leaves us in chaos. Yet
these same conditions invite us to make of ourselves and our
lives what we will, to experience the satisfactions often found in
love and work. *Crisis in Intimacy* invites you to explore the
richness life has to offer.

In our continuous search for values and guidelines, we want
to find an ethical system appropriate to our modern world and
the context in which we live. The primary purpose of this book is
to help readers formulate personal guidelines that will enhance
their relationships and their lives. *Crisis in Intimacy* is appropriate for use alone, as a supplementary text, for courses in marriage and family counseling, human sexuality, and personal or
adult development.

A sense of self-worth requires us to maintain a responsible
standard of behavior. Responsibility—the ability to fulfill one's
needs in a way that does not deprive others of fulfilling theirs—
can lead each of us toward greater satisfaction. Finding such a
path requires us to open our minds, to see things the way they
are, to explore and question, to absorb information, and to use
our personal experiences in ways that will enrich our lives and
the lives of those we love.

In these pages, we explore human relationships—with the
self, with others, and with work. Those who expect to find "the
answer," like a map that plots "the way" to happiness ever after,

will be disappointed. Most of our suffering is self-created through our impossible demand for certainty. Answers are not found in books but created and re-created within persons. Exploring relationships is a search down a long road that never ends, a challenge, and a lifelong quest.

Although our relationships are personal, they must be understood in a social context that exists within a particular culture. Today, we find many people in a state of confusion and disillusionment about relationships. Feelings of discomfort, disenchantment, and alienation have reached epidemic proportions. In our relationships, we are experiencing a crisis.

*Crisis in Intimacy* suggests this crisis is partly the result of illusions and fantasies about what relationships "should" be. Expectations, both learned and chosen, often destroy human relationships. We can, instead, become more aware of the pervasive contradictions and paradoxes occurring within ourselves and our culture.

We often think that, given enough information, both theoretical and experiential, we can choose personal and relevant ways to relate to ourselves and to one another. Reading about relationships, however, is like reading about playing the piano. Reading by itself is not enough. Growth, awareness, and change in relationships require a commitment of time, thought, and energy. Therefore, those readers who are willing to write down pertinent thoughts or insights that come to mind as well as to work on the exercises and questions in the book stand to benefit the most.

Some theories will be more useful and helpful to one person than to others; hence, theories from many different disciplines, such as sociology, psychology, anthropology, and philosophy, are included here. Each person can select from those presented to create personal theories. These will change, however, with different relationships and at different times in the life cycle. Relationships are constantly changing.

This book is *not* a psychological "tool box" to reach into, or a bag of gimmicks or tricks to use; it is *not* a "how to improve your relationships" manual; yet at times, the reader may find a thought or an ideal that has value. Rather than offer prescriptions, this book explores possibilities and acknowledges that many of our views will be transformed tomorrow.

*Crisis in Intimacy* offers a foundation on which to build relationships with the self and others. One difficulty with this is that often we value what we have been taught is valuable. Our thoughts and feelings are rarely our own. But we can learn to catch ourselves acting out old assumptions. We can create new self-definitions and values by becoming more aware of our own traps—the ways we use language, stock responses, habit patterns that manipulate ourselves and others. We can learn to enhance rather than to interfere with our own personal growth and the growth of others.

*Crisis in Intimacy* explores the concept that there is no "right" way to live that eliminates responsible choice. Each of us must establish and reestablish guidelines over and over, throughout the many stages of our lives. Questions and exercises offer the reader an opportunity to explore personal transitions and changing values and to cut through self-deception.

In *Crisis in Intimacy*, I suggest that most of us live with certain human conditions: chronic dissatisfaction, vague feelings of emptiness, unwillingness to tolerate distress, yearning for a soul mate, longing to love and be loved, wanting to be connected to something larger than the self, and searching for meaning in life. These conditions can give us energy and the drive to change, act, grow, and fulfill our human potential.

In these pages, I encourage the reader to experience fear and anxiety as parts of the human condition that can provide a stronger foundation from which to function. Life without change, without mystery, would be dull and boring. From a mix of magic, confusion, pain, and wonder, life offers us a banquet.

Through the transformation process, each of us has the capacity to find our personal place beyond where we are today. The person who develops an openness to change, an exploration of paradox, and an attention to new experiences learns to free the self and create a new perception of human potential. To these ends, *Crisis in Intimacy* is dedicated.

Every published work reflects the contributions of many people. I am grateful for the suggestions provided by the following manuscript reviewers: Luther Baker, Central Washington University; M. Betsy Bergen, Kansas State University; John Brennecke, Mt. San Antonio College; Robert Burgess, Pennsylvania State University; and Jeffrey Flatt, Westfield State College. I also want to thank Linda Ruth Wright and Phyllis Larimore for their editorial help. And most important, I appreciate Claire Verduin, sponsoring editor, for her personal attention and support.

*Jacquelyn B. Carr*

# Contents

# Crisis in Intimacy

# The Crisis in Intimacy 1

*The world we have made as a result of the
level of thinking we have done thus far creates
problems we cannot solve at the same level at
which we created them.*

*Einstein*

Although, at times, we believe world discord comes from political or economic situations, underlying these global problems is how human beings relate to one another. Human relationships are the foundation for the most important aspects of our lives.

Consciously or unconsciously, we spend our lives searching for guidelines that will help us live in harmony with others. We sense that what matters most in an individual life is the imprint of love we leave behind us. Of all the many kinds of human love, man–woman relationships, sex, and parenthood are universal and timeless.

Today, these relationships differ from those our parents experienced partly because the present social context differs significantly from that of the past. Moreover, as each of us matures, our values about relationships change. Therefore, we all must constantly reassess our personal relationships.

Our culture is rapidly changing. The constant revision of moral rules and social standards leaves us with too many paths that lead in opposing directions. Traditionally, women were conditioned to be passive, dependent, vulnerable, and insecure. Men were conditioned to be aggressive, strong, emotionally closed, and work oriented.

Today, many women want equality, autonomy, and independence, and many men want an intellectual companion and friend who will share the financial responsibilities of supporting the family. However, both women and men seem unaware of the price and unprepared for the tradeoffs in these changing roles.

Bewildered and anxious about ever knowing what is the "right" thing to do or the "best" way to go, we may strongly desire, at times, to say, "I don't want to play." But not playing does not work. It is not an alternative.

Like ostriches that bury their heads in the sand and believe themselves unseen, each of us, at times, wants to avoid life by refusing to face it. Eventually, we have to come up for air. No decision is a decision not to decide, for which each of us is personally responsible.

External changes in our lives seem less threatening when we have a consistent or dependable philosophical basis for handling our human relationships. Since no universal set of rules can provide guidelines for everyone, each person must turn inward to find his or her own answers.

Many people say they hunger for authentic, intimate, long-lasting relationships. They want love and respect. They want to make human relationships work. Yet we live in impersonal communities, often lacking the protection or concern of neighbors. We depend on a mechanized society that separates us from any direct or personal contact with those who make the products we consume. Thus we often feel as if we lack communion with other human beings.

When cultural values center on acquisitions, success, or financial security, we tend to follow other-directed paths. In superficial human contacts, we feel discomfort as we pretend to be different from who we are. This lack of authenticity we experience as a *crisis in intimacy.*

## What Is a Crisis?

Anthropologists tell us stages of growth occur in every culture—birth, puberty, marriage, parenthood, old age, death. Primitive cultures have ceremonies to ease the pain of these transitions. Complex societies, however, tend to ignore these rites of passage. When we neglect or shorten these ceremonies, we feel disoriented and unprepared for the next stage in life.

*A crisis may occur at a social or personal turning point, an emotionally significant event, or a radical change of status.* At a time of crisis, a pivotal decision must be made to travel in one direction or another.

Adolescents experience moodiness and emotional instability. Their bodies change rapidly. At times, they feel as if they are inside a physical shell that does not belong to them. Suddenly, they have hair in unfamiliar places, body odors, voice changes, and different-looking skin and teeth. They are several inches taller and have added 25 or 30 pounds to their body weight in a year.

These physical changes, often accompanied by the pain of self-consciousness and daily anxieties, occur just when the individual wants to attract members of the opposite sex. An adolescent often feels ugly or stupid when being attractive, getting good grades, and impressing others are vitally important. The passage through puberty is a classic *crisis* with its pain, growth, and change. However, even if it were possible, few of us would choose to avoid or skip life's transitions.

In today's complex society, we have periods of crisis other than those recognized by anthropologists. Marriage, children leaving home, divorce, loss of a job, and retirement are all crises.

A crisis is *not* a catastrophe like an earthquake or a tragedy like the untimely death of a loved one. A crisis is a time of confusion connected with some change that does not have a design, pattern, or single "right" path to follow.

A few decades ago, most people walked similar roads: education, marriage, children, family, one job until retirement. Today, many people change careers or professions, move from one city or state to another, begin and end relationships. These changes require new ways of thinking about transitions.

Thomas Paine said, "The nearer any disease approaches to a crisis, the nearer it is to a cure." These decisive or vital stages marked by turning points are a normal and natural part of human existence, yet we seldom know what to do when they happen. Transitions often occur on some unconscious level. Unaware of our changes, we often recognize them only in retrospect.

The experience of crisis gives a message, "Let go." We often identify with something from the past, something too small for us in the present. Letting go of who we were or what we valued is often painful—particularly when it affects others. When our lives are quiet or dull, we look back on turbulent times with a wistful, sometimes sentimental, yearning to return and relive that excitement. With nostalgia, we recall the first time we left home, the first few months after marriage, or the first weeks after the birth of our son or daughter.

Often during these transitions, we felt confused and anxious. Yet we not only got through them, we triumphed and grew beyond them. Within each of us lie untapped wellsprings of strength that sustain us in times of change.

Sometimes we create a crisis so that we can experience something that will increase our sense of personal worth and help us grow. We want an invigorating, exciting life. We actually seek the stimulation of variety while we want the safety of sameness.

In Chinese, the word *crisis* is made up of two equal symbols: danger and opportunity. Life offers few opportunities for change without some danger. Opportunity means risking pain for the rewards of growth. Although we sometimes want to retreat, to go back to what is familiar, *to be alive is to change.*

## Sources of Crisis

One of the primary sources of crisis is in the tension between two opposing forces. We have a need to know ourselves, but at the same time, we are afraid to look. The tension between the need to know and the fear of knowing presents us with an insoluble dilemma. The paradox is the more intimate we become with ourselves, the less fearful we are. Before we can establish a foundation for intimacy in our relationships with others, we must be familiar with, close to, and knowledgeable about ourselves.

A second source of crisis is in the tension between wanting to be close to others and wanting to be free. *We fear loneliness.* Although all of us, at times, need to be alone, to be quiet, to be creative, to gain wisdom about life, and to understand ourselves, we fear being cut off, isolated, and unconnected from others.

This fear of separateness results in a longing to be one with another human being. We search for that perfect mate who will protect us from loneliness. We want to deny that each of us is a separate entity, so we devise all sorts of methods for unity, communion, community—any momentary physical, emotional, or spiritual experience to deny separateness.

We live in an uprooted time, so feeling as if no one cares is not uncommon. We feel estranged, separate, disconnected, and frightened. We believe loneliness can be avoided by anchoring our life to another person's in a relationship. Not knowing who we are or what we are searching for, we hope to discover what we feel and think through reflections mirrored from another person.

In a desperate search for intimacy and burdened by the myths of romantic love, we want to belong to someone who knows our deepest nature and is concerned about us, someone who will tell us what to do and protect us in crises.

We want more than simple companionship and mutual support. We want lifelong guarantees. Yet being connected to another person often leads to feeling trapped. We resent our loss of freedom, and when we resent someone whom we love and who loves us, we feel guilt.

To summarize, sources of crisis are

- A drive to change accompanied by a resistance to change
- A drive toward self-knowledge accompanied by a resistance to self-awareness
- A drive for unity or closeness with others accompanied by a resistance to connections that rob us of freedom
- A drive for safety accompanied by a desire for the excitement and adventure of the unknown

Ralph Waldo Emerson said, "As soon as there is life, there is danger." As soon as there is danger, the most fundamental human impulse is to create security. The widespread preoccupation with safety creates anxiety. Government efforts to create national security, for example, result in international paranoia. Paradoxically, then, the quest for security results in feeling insecure.

Changes—simultaneously exciting and frightening—require that we give up comfortable, safe responses and tolerate feeling vulnerable and insecure. Eventually, we learn that *security can not be found externally* in other people, things, or conditions.

Personal, social, and cultural transitions provide us with stimulation. Each of us can set the quantity and quality of change in our personal lives, but some stress accompanies most decisions. A certain amount of stress is the spice of life. Without it, we would be either vegetables or dead.

One person thrives on stress, whereas another can hardly bear it. Managing stress and change is a personal challenge that each of us can meet through constant self-questioning and self-evaluation.

More important than answers, questions lead us to explore, to find tentative guidelines, suggestions, and possibilities. We can learn to operate in a *surveillance mode* rather than a problem-solving mode. Instead of gathering information to make choices among alternatives, we scan our environments for surprises and solutions. We can simply monitor, like a participant-observer, what is going on both in the environment and within ourselves.

Scanning calls for gathering a lot of information, even information that might appear irrelevant to decision makers who operate by applying rules and copying others' solutions. Most information comes to us through the biases of others and is tainted by how it is generated. Even in scientific research, information is biased.

Highly regarded advice and generally accepted facts can be misleading. So-called good advice and reliable information may be inappropriate for a particular person, situation, or time. The responsibility for gathering and interpreting data belongs to each of us. As we search for personal alternatives and new objectives in life, we can reinterpret the ambiguous past in the light of our personal views of the world.

Ultimately, crises spring primarily from personal interpretations. As we experience what today's choices bring, we make decisions that give us more information. Although a relationship continues with the same person and a job with the same company, the relationship and the job change as we and the people around us change. The illusion of sameness often comes from inattention or unawareness used as a defense against acknowledging change.

## What Is Intimacy?

Like most words that are only symbols for ideas, the word *intimacy* has many meanings depending on the context in which it is used. Intimacy with the self is *that state in which a person is aware of the inmost character of his or her self—those most fundamental, essential, and private parts.*

In the study of relationships among people, the word *intimate* pertains to *close personal relations characterized by warm friendship; private or closely personal.* Intimacy may sprout suddenly from a chance meeting with a stranger, but it must be nurtured over time for it to grow. Through close relationships, we learn to care for others and be cared for in return.

Another kind of intimacy occurs in a romantic relationship where we share *the most inner, personal, deep, intrinsic parts of ourselves with those innermost parts of another.* The most intimate romantic relationships include a joining of bodies, minds, feelings, and spirits.

The fear of separation often leads us to search for closeness with others. Paradoxically, we fear that in union with another person we will lose ourselves, that our identity will be submerged. Psychotherapist Karen Horney believes the source of anxiety lies in our selfish, hostile impulses. We suffer guilt and fear when we wish another person harm or punishment. We also fear they have hostile impulses toward us. Thus to protect ourselves from separation and harm, we search for unity with another person.

The search for intimacy, then, is supposedly an antidote to such human conditions as loneliness and hostility. We hope sharing our life with a compatible companion—one with whom we can share mutual affection and trust—will protect us from our separateness, from hostility and injustice.

Some psychologists believe intimacy is not so much a matter of what or how much is shared as it is *the degree of mutual need-satisfaction within the relationship.* Yet we run into insoluble problems when we expect someone else to satisfy our needs. Skating back and forth between her needs and his needs is rarely coordinated. Sometimes when one person wants to talk the other wants to sleep. Thus the concept of intimacy as need-satisfaction has limits.

Often conflicts between the differing desires of two persons prevent intimacy. Therefore, most of us, at times in our lives, choose separateness because of the risks and tensions in both conflict and interdependency. Wanting closeness and distance simultaneously presents us with an insoluble dilemma. The message we send is "Go away a little closer."

Intimacy at its best is a reciprocal expression of feeling and thought, not out of fear or dependent need, but out of a wish to know another's inner life and to be able to share one's own. We yearn to discard the masks we wear. Though we hunger to be ourselves, we fear rejection. At times, we even have difficulty believing ourselves lovable.

One barrier to intimacy is connected to the differences in how women and men deal with their inner emotional lives. Generally, women are more able to locate, describe, and define an emotion they feel. A man, however, when asked, "What are you feeling right now?" is often puzzled and may answer, "Just what I was telling you" or "I don't know."

Women also are usually more verbal. Physical closeness with silence isolates them. For many men, nonverbal closeness is often enough; they feel reassured simply having a woman available when needed. But a woman wants more. She not only wants a man to be open with her, she wants him to want her to be open with him. For a woman, intimacy is the desire to know another's inner life along with the ability to share one's own.

To establish his male identity, a man tries to renounce his connection with mother need-dependency and vulnerability to a woman. At the same time, he hungers for a female mate. Women, too, are apprehensive about intimacy. They sense when a relationship feels uncomfortable, but seldom understand why or what to do about it.

When relationships are unsatisfactory, both men and women create checklists of things to blame: He or she is too short/tall, too smart/dumb, too young/old, too passive/aggressive, too needy/self-contained. The longing continues for the perfect soul mate to come find us.

The more desperately we search for intimacy, the less real is our ability to satisfy it. We want closeness, but we dread being absorbed by it. *Intimacy has a high price;* it requires a willingness to be vulnerable, to express power and tenderness alike, to respond as both male and female within one body.

Sometimes we mistake other qualities in a person for intimacy. A woman with outstanding social skills and little sense of privacy walks into a room of strangers radiating warmth and openness. She attracts many people to her. Although she is willing to tell others about her feelings and experiences, she has no intention of getting close to any single person.

Nurturance is another quality often confused with intimacy. Like caretaking, nurturance binds others to us and ensures against the pain of loneliness. It promises selfless giving and generosity. Some men, as well as many women, offer nurturance that makes those around them dependent. They dominate others through giving. Emotional or financial dependence may offer safety and security but not intimacy.

Another paradox is that intimacy restricts us at the same time it expands us. Intimacy requires that we give up freedom, that we compromise our individuality as we fuse our identity with another's. Maintaining a separate identity in the context of an intimate relationship is the prevailing concern today—one to be wrestled with again and again.

The crisis in intimacy often stems from male–female differences, ambivalence, and fear of change. To welcome change as a "dangerous opportunity" is difficult in a culture that teaches us to avoid danger, to "play it cool," and above all, to "play it safe."

We have great difficulty understanding and coping with ambivalence—the coexistence of opposite feelings about the same person or object. Our education system, based on logic, does not help us when we both love *and* resent a person. Ambivalent feelings are incomprehensible when we try to understand them through logic. We sometimes solve this dilemma through fantasy.

Human actions, thoughts, and feelings are rarely consistent. Yet the need for consistency—for making new information fit with old information—often results in cognitive dissonance. We usually strive to reduce this tension between new ideas and old beliefs. What we do not understand, we fear; what might change us, we disagree with.

The continual effort to make one's world view emotionally, if not logically, consistent is called *psychologic*. This drive for consistency often prompts us to deceive ourselves. Each of us chooses the degree of consistency that feels comfortable and lives with both the favorable and the unfavorable aspects of our choices.

For some, fantasy is more beautiful than reality. The source of fantasy is *the Ideal*—what life would be like if we were complete and our world were perfect. Although fantasies may provide some persons with ways of coping, others suffer disillusionment. To find personal freedom, we can explore the discrepancies between our dreams and expectations. On this journey, some points of focus in this book are

- To look at what is happening in our lives and in our world
- To become more conscious of discrepancies between the ideal and the real
- To look at the social origins of personal ambivalence and paradox

- To look at the processes of self-definition, self-deception, and the role of language in these processes
- To review how we choose partners or companions and how we interact with them
- To review the fact that intimacy means conflict
- To explore ways to reorder priorities as we experience the transformations that are part of being human
- To create a personal philosophy that can bring satisfaction to our lives

Throughout this book, we expand the concepts and definitions of intimacy—with the self and others—by exploring the connections between intimacy and deception, attraction, love, marriage, sex, resentment, and work.

The quest for fulfillment in life begins as a personal search. Self-acceptance, a prerequisite to rewarding human relationships, is characterized by warmth and friendship. Ultimately, each of us wants to make a contribution, a commitment to and a connection with the society we live in. We want to make a difference in the world.

Our culture provides us with a setting for our assumptions, expectations, and values about relationships. In the process of socialization, we are often personally rewarded when we act out of consideration for the welfare of others. We experience trust, faith in being human, and an altruistic selfishness that benefits us all. Each of us can aspire to leave the world a better place.

# *Intimacy and the Self*   2

*The true vocation of man
is to find his way to
himself.*

Hermann Hesse

M ost human beings hunger for closeness with others. As infants, we experienced feelings of warmth and caring, and we want to reexperience those safe feelings of our early life. The word *intimate* pertains to the *inmost character of a thing;* it means *fundamental, essential, most private or personal.*

To experience intimacy, understanding the fundamental nature of the *self* is essential. In most of us, there is some tension between the need to know the self and the fear of knowing the self. To some extent, most of us are afraid that if we look, we might find something threatening, unlikable, or unacceptable. At the same time, we find self-exploration, with its risk of learning something new, exciting.

Psychologists say we will see only what we are ready to see. We have certain methods of defending ourselves. We use many self-deceptive techniques to escape reality and protect our self-image. Therefore, searching for personal insights is relatively safe although not always comfortable. Sigmund Freud defined and described defense mechanisms such as repression, projection, and rationalization, which we explore in Chapter 3. In this chapter, we focus on self-discovery, which includes both anxiety and excitement.

Each of us begins life in close association with others. We learn how to be human among other humans. Intimate also means *closely acquainted or associated; very familiar.* Thus we learn to be intimate with the self. Intimacy costs something. It makes us vulnerable. Piaget, the child psychologist, tells us children construct reality from perceptions created through the process of socialization. Thus self-image and the needs allied with it are learned from others.

## Self-Concept

The child transcends his purely physical existence as self-awareness develops. A tiny infant begins as a center of sensations, slowly acquiring an awareness of a self endowed with certain capacities. The infant begins to differentiate self from things not self as he or she learns the ball, the spoon, the cup are objects outside the self. Then, gradually, internal sensations are sorted out. The child learns to attach different meanings to being hungry and being full, being dry and being wet. The self becomes identified as something that feels, wants, and does things.

As we learn language, we learn to name people—mommy, daddy, baby. We then begin to learn "good" comes with a kiss, hug, or smile. And "bad" comes with a frown or slap. With the expression "good baby," we perceive a self that has certain characteristics. Before we are a year old, we learn being good is rewarded with love.

Mommy and daddy are separate from self. The consciousness of self is not innate but learned. A child constructs a self-image through interaction with others in a world structured by language.

Self-concept is mainly a product of our past communications and relations with others in our family. We create ourselves largely from what we believe others have perceived of us. Although our self-image is forever changing, its greatest development occurs in childhood.

The problem of defining the self is essentially that of defining the word *I*. We assume we know who we are, but we find it difficult to describe ourselves. Although we create our own self-image, we depend on others to reflect back to us some confirmation beyond our own perceptions.

John Locke said,

Self is that conscious thinking thing which is sensible or conscious of pleasure and pain, capable of happiness or misery, and so is concerned for itself, as far as that consciousness extends.

A broader definition would also include *the sum total of all that a person calls his or her own*, including loved ones, personal property, and experiences.

The self is that aspect of you that determines your uniqueness as a separate entity from "not self," from the environment and all that is outside self. The self can never be fully known because it is constantly changing. Yet it is in the family that we first begin to experience the concept of self.

## The Family

To create a self, we depend on the family. Some families give permission to carry memories by telling family stories. Grandparents pass family history from one generation to the next. Self-concept is unconsciously affected by identifying with family origins. Tracing our family history can give us insight into how we define ourselves.

---

Looking at family roots can give us some clues to self-identity.

- What are the roots of your family name? Where do your grandparents come from? What countries represent the family? What regions of the country?
- Imagine yourself as one of your grandparents. Go back to the time in which he or she was born. What was the world like? What kind of a house did they live in? What kinds of clothes did they wear? What kind of an education did they have? Imagine yourself living in their time as if you were one of your grandparents.
- How far back do you remember? What is your first memory?
- What is your first memory of your mother? Your father?
- Who takes responsibility for family memories?
- Who saves photographs and keeps records and other objects (family bible, marriage licenses, birth certificates, and so on)?
- Are there family memory taboos (subjects no one discusses, skeletons in the family closet)?

---

Most of us are unaware of the power of our past. But through exploring our past—even beyond our grandparents' time—we can discover a whole world we unconsciously identify with.

### Selective Memory

We have a tendency to forget some things and exaggerate others. Psychologists call this selective memory. We often forget unpleasant experiences and remember pleasant ones. We usually remember what we believe is important, what interests us, and what makes sense to us. We remember what we are motivated to remember. If we have memories that do not fit our self-image, we distort them for the sake of consistency and logic. We want very much to experience the security that comes from knowing who we are, so we actually create our past.

The past you remember is not what really happened. The family experiences you have saved in your memory were probably much different from what you remember. Yet we often act as if the memories we have conceived actually happened. Then we get emotionally invested in our own stories.

One way to test this theory is to get together with other family members and ask, "What do you remember about the time when we lived in the big house on Stanyan Street?" Or "Do you remember at John's wedding when . . . ?" As you listen, do not judge the discrepancies between your memories and theirs. What we tell one another of what we remember says more about the person remembering than about the event remembered.

Most of us are convinced our own memories are infallible, that the memories others have that are different from ours are simple distortions if not downright lies. We tend to create the story of our life by selecting bits and pieces that justify our images of ourselves and others. Each time we tell our story, even if only to ourselves, we reinforce the images. Thus we make up the good guys and bad guys, the events, and the dialogue.

---

Exploring your past self can help you discover how you constructed your present self-image.

- Order of birth or position in the family (first, middle, last, or only child) affects self-image. How did your position in the family affect you?
- Write three advantages of being born in the family position you occupy. Write three disadvantages.
- If you had a choice, would you switch positions?

Exploring past relationships with parents, siblings, grand-parents, and other family members can reap great rewards in self-understanding and awareness. A bonus of this exploration is that you can sometimes change inappropriate past behaviors you continue to act out in present relationships.

Each of us has thousands of hours of "memory tapes" that were "recorded" from our childhood and still lie dormant in our memories. Close your eyes and try to visualize a scene from your childhood. Listen to the voice of one of your parents. Do you hear words like "stupid," "smart," "good," or "pretty"? What do you say to yourself, today, when you make a mistake or are pleased with something you have done? Most of us echo those evaluations from our childhood.

Self-image is partly based on the labels we selected from the many we heard as children. When Mary was 3 years old, she heard her mother say, "Mary is shy." Mary experienced herself as looking at the floor, holding her mother's hand, and being quiet. She connected this behavior with the word *shy*. Now, years later, Mary says to herself, "I am shy." This label becomes a self-fulfilling prophecy. Each of us labels ourselves—life of the party, loyal, docile, good-natured, aggressive or passive, strong or weak—then we play out these labels as if they were who we are. Language becomes a prison in which we act out what we tell ourselves we are.

When we become conscious of this labeling, we can retain the satisfying labels and change those that are not. Criticism and compliments from the past become a part of our present. Those judgments we heard as children become personal prop-erty: "I'm not very good in math," "I've always been a lousy speller." Then we have the satisfaction of proving we are right by making mistakes in math and spelling.

---

Whenever you feel negative about yourself, sit down and write three positive things about yourself.

If you want some control over your performance, you can change your negative statements into positive ones:

- "I am better at math this year than last year."
- "I can spell better now than I could six months ago."

This process can change both your performance and self-image. If you continually say unfavorable things about your self, ask, "What do I gain when I belittle myself?"

---

Sometimes continuing a negative habit results in a feeling of stability, the assurance of consistency. We create our own self-images.

Each of us has layers of self-perception. Like an onion, these layers can be peeled off one by one. Some of these layers may be positive, others negative. Like masks, we hide behind them. Somewhere at the core lies the essence of our natural being covered by layers of family, social, and cultural programming.

---

As you answer the following questions, do so without censoring or judging yourself. Write freely for as long as you can.

- "Who am I?"
- "Who do I pretend to be?"
- "Who do I wish to be?"

When repeated at intervals, this exercise can give you new insights into yourself. You need not alter how you feel or think. Simply look, explore, and enjoy.

---

### The Omnipotent Parent Illusion

When you were small, you thought your parents had total control over you. Actually, parents have little control of how a child *perceives* what a parent says or intends. Thus a child's self-concept is not simply the result of what parents do or say. For example, one child will consider an authoritarian parent loving, another will consider the parent a prison guard.

Even the form of rebellion a child chooses is not under parental control. One child will fight verbally, and another physically, while a third child wins with passive withdrawal or inattention. Parents simply do not have as much control as we have been led to believe. One advantage of thinking parents are omnipotent is that by blaming them, we can pretend we are not responsible for our own self-concept or personality.

Each of us grows up with a parent voice in our heads. As

adults, we may unconsciously use this voice to get ourselves to behave in certain ways. Self-manipulation is common. We threaten, preach, praise, lecture, judge, examine, and scold ourselves. So ingrained are some of these voices that we use them in our other relationships.

If we had a "helper" parent, one who manipulated us with praise, we may use positive judgments to get ourselves and others to do what we want. "That's a good job" or "You're a good person" both set guidelines for the kinds of behavior we expect from others.

---

Recall the positive and negative techniques used in your family to teach values and control behavior.

- List some things you were told to do or be ("Be polite," "Be considerate," "Be quiet," "Be clean").
- List some things you were told *not* to do or be ("Don't touch," "Don't cry," "Don't stare").
- Make separate lists of things your mother wanted and your father wanted.
- Write about a major event in your childhood that was happy. Write about a major event that was sad.
- Write about your most embarrassing experience.
- Write about a childhood disappointment.
- Write about a time when you felt very good about yourself.
- Write about a time when you felt you were bad.
- Write about a person who was very important to you.

---

In 1986, the first major results to emerge from a long-term project at the University of Minnesota indicate that personality traits are primarily inherited. More than 350 pairs of twins went through extensive testing over seven years. The identical twins studied included some who were reared in different families. If environment were the dominant influence in personality, identical twins raised in the same home would be expected to show more similarity than those raised apart. But the researchers found the child's genetic makeup has a stronger influence on personality than the child's upbringing. These findings shatter a widespread belief in the primacy of family influence.

Whether you want to blame your parents or credit your genes, whatever distorted perceptions, painful experiences, or imperfect reflections you had as a child, today, as an adult, you have the power to change your attitudes toward yourself and create a new self-concept.

Whatever you did to be noticed, accepted, or loved by your parents you may do today to gain the approval of friends and acquaintances. These habitual responses are often unconscious. To become more aware of them, try to think about what you do and why you do it. Those habits that are unproductive you can change.

### Other Significant Family Members

Other significant persons in our past lives such as brothers and sisters, grandparents, and teachers also influenced our values and self-images. Sibling relationships—sister to sister, brother to brother, and sister to brother—contribute dramatically to our initial sense of self and have a lifelong impact.

In a study of the relationship between birth order and personality, a team of behavioral scientists from the University of Florida found that oldest children tend to feel dethroned by the birth of a younger brother or sister and respond by trying to regain their importance. The result is often persons who strive for power and recognition. Youngest children of course are never dethroned and tend to be pampered and spoiled, resulting in charming, sociable, dependent behavior. Middle children tend to develop skills in compromise and diplomacy. Although our knowledge about the relationship between birth order and personality is imprecise, it still can help us identify and change behavior patterns.

Some memories sustain us while others fester. There are wounds and gifts, selfish betrayals and generous confidences, understandings and misunderstandings so fundamental that they influence our expectations in every relationship that follows. Though the intimacies of childhood may seem to disintegrate, the pull to recover them may later emerge in forms we do not recognize. Exploring family ties proves valuable in understanding adult relationships. One woman writes:

> My sister was born two years and ten months after I was born. She was a sickly baby. My mother spent every minute worrying about and holding the new baby. My mother often sent me to my grandmother's. Years later, I understood how much the experience of a sickly baby sister affected me. When my own children were born, even though they were healthy, I was terrified they would die.

As an adult, I continue to feel maternal and protective of my "baby" sister at the same time I reexperience sibling jealousy. Although as an adult I *know* it was not so, I still feel as if my mother loved the baby best. This ambivalence of loving protectiveness and competitive jealousy not only affected my relationship with my sister but affects other relationships as well.

Most of us tend to create "movies" about our lives, with family members playing stereotyped dramatic roles. We have rewritten the script from selected incidents often unrelated to what actually happened or the real people, who neither good nor bad, are simply human beings with different perceptions of themselves, us, past experiences and relationships.

We have selectively assembled images of parents and siblings based on past impressions and experiences. These images are simplistic and distorted; often we reconstruct only half a person, such as someone who is all bad or all good.

---

Rewriting past images of family members can free us to relate to them as they are now.

- If you tend to describe your mother's negative qualities, write a positive description. If you tend to paint a positive picture of your mother, write about some of her weaknesses. Do the same for your father.
- If you have a brother or sister, do the same for them.
- Grandparents sometimes play a vital role in the family. If your grandmother or grandfather played an important role, explore his or her influences on your self-image.

This exercise will help you unify these two halves into a more realistic whole person who has less power over your current relationships.

---

One of the greatest forces in our lives is expectations. What we expect from life or what we want often controls us. For example, children born without siblings often fantasize about an imaginary brother or sister. One woman who was an only child tells how much she missed not having a sister. She goes through life searching among friends for the sister she never had. Most of us have some images of what we wanted when we were children that we did not get. These images often become drives in adulthood.

---

We often create what we think we missed as children to give us some direction as adults.

- What were some of the things you feel you missed when you were growing up? Be as specific as you can; for example, "I wanted to go to the circus, but my father said, 'no.' "
- Did this unfulfilled expectation result in your seeing yourself as deprived? Do you still use this image of the deprived child today?

---

We become comfortable with the stability of the family roles we played as children and tend to carry them into later relationships. A man with older sisters often finds himself drawn to women who mother or boss him. The man with a younger sister whom he teased tends to relate to women by teasing them. Children without siblings may have trouble, as adults, sharing space or "toys" or making compromises. Becoming aware of the influences of childhood can give us more choices about how we want to relate to others as adults.

### Changing Images

Direct correlations may or may not exist between the images you have of family members and who they really are. As children, we considered our parents omnipotent. One young man tells a story about his mother:

> When I was about 5 years old, my mother always knew everything I had done, like getting into the cookie jar. When I was accused, I would ask her how she knew. She told me, "A little birdie told me." For years, I believed there was a little bird who followed me around and reported back to my mother.

One of the tasks of adolescence is to mourn the death of our omnipotent parents. During this time—this process—our disappointment often turns to anger; it is as if we were duped or conned. Not one person ever grows to adulthood having all wants gratified. Each of us enters adulthood feeling somehow slighted or wronged. We feel that a parent or sibling has been insensitive or that there was something we did not get. Considering our unrealistic expectations, it is doubtful whether a single adult feels he has had enough love. Most of us feel we have a right to total fulfillment and unconditional love, and it is someone else's responsibility to give it to us.

---

Recalling past pain and the sources we blame can be valuable.

- Recall a time your mother hurt your feelings. What happened and what was said? Recall a time your father hurt your feelings. What happened and what was said?
- What, in each parent separately, do you resent more than anything else?
- What did your mother do that you do not want to forgive? What did your father do that you do not want to forgive?
- Was there something you expected from your mother you did not get? Do you feel your mother loved you enough? Was there something you expected from your father you did not get? Do you feel your father loved you enough?

    Look at your true feelings and express them without reservation or judging yourself. Then let them go.

---

    As children, we are fully aware of our dependence on our parents for physical and emotional sustenance. We perceive them as *the providers of all satisfactions and the righters of all wrongs.* But we also experience them as the ones who impose restrictions and punishments. Because we, at once, love, fear, and resent them, we endure the most wrenching of all feelings—ambivalence.

    Simultaneously, we love and hate our parents. But as babies, we soon learn we are not allowed to bite or hit them. We learn it is unacceptable to be angry with them. We are told how bad it is to not totally love our parents who totally love us.

    Not loving your own child or your own parent is sacrilegious. Parents and children seek self-love through each other, as if existence itself depends on the other's love. We struggle to be perfect parents and perfect children, to earn what we do not feel we deserve. The illusion is that we can get from others what we have been unable to give ourselves. And the paradox is that the parent who gives up his or her life out of love for a child loses both. No one wants the burden of or responsibility for another's life.

Since parents are inevitably stronger and more skillful than children, parent worshiping may continue too long. A child may feel incapable of ever attaining the parent's perfection. But the time does come when, as adolescents, we realize our childhood images are faulty. Our parents, we see, are human beings with weaknesses. They are not omnipotent, and we may never forgive them for not being what we created. The loss of that ideal parent leaves many adolescents mourning for years. Others are so angry that their rebellion overwhelms the entire family. These young people may spend years punishing their parents for being imperfect.

If we ignore these illusions of deprivation or of having been ill-treated in some way as a child, they can have great power over our adult relationships. However, we can diffuse them by learning how *to give ourselves the love we wanted*. When we expect others to fulfill our needs, we create our own unhappiness. We can exist without total fulfillment and be comfortable in situations that, at times, seem disorderly, uncertain, or even inaccurate.

Because we want to think of ourselves as consistent and dependable, we tend to lock into old self-images. We cling to old angers and resentments. Often, we act like who we were rather than who we are. We do not want others to change either, so we treat them as they were in the past rather than as they are today. Then, they too seem trapped in old roles, responding as they used to be, and preventing the relationship from changing. Nowhere are these old patterned responses more evident than when an adult child, home to visit his or her parents, becomes trapped in past interaction patterns.

---

The capacity to deal with change in ourselves, others, and relationships is essential to personal growth.

- Visualize yourself as you were ten years ago. Notice how you dressed, talked, and acted. Looking at old photographs might help. Who were your friends? Whom were you living with? What kind of car were you driving? What was your house like?
- Now visualize yourself as you are today. How do you dress,

talk, and act? What do you do each day? Whom do you spend time with now? What kind of car do you drive? What is your living situation like? Dwell on the changes.
- Now visualize yourself as you will be in ten years. What kind of work are you doing? What kind of car are you driving? Whom do you live with? What kinds of clothes do you wear? Who are your friends? What kinds of relationships do you have?

---

It may be harder for some people than for others to break out of old patterns and self-images. In trying to be consistent and to stay the same, we use language. The use of the *to be* verbs (is, are, was, were) locks people in and defines them as objects. "I am honest" or "I am dependable" sound unauthentic. Although we may want to be more honest than we, at times, have been, we cannot *be honest*, just as we cannot be a rock. People change to fit their circumstances. To be rigid, to define oneself as a thing is a pretense, an attempt to be consistent.

Sometimes we define ourselves by what we do for a living. "I am a teacher (mechanic, engineer)" contributes only a shred of information about us. Sometimes we define ourselves by some act or behavior. Instead of saying, "I am impotent (frigid)," say, "In the last few weeks (or months), I have been unable to have an orgasm." The act or the lack of it does not define you and is not a permanent state. Instead of saying "I am a homosexual" (like a table or chair), say, "At this time in my life, I prefer people of my own sex." We can learn to use language more accurately and to recognize that the language we use to define ourselves can be misleading.

Each day our cells grow and change, and our bodies, emotions, thoughts, and language change. The world all around us changes. Being able to deal with change in ourselves and others results in personal growth. A person stagnates when behavior and goals remain the same. Fear of change can be overcome. We can find enjoyment in discovering differences between today and yesterday as well as in exploring possibilities in tomorrow. If you spend a few minutes every month or so asking yourself how you and others are changing, you will be more conscious of the differences.

One of the hazards of being a parent is that by the time you have figured out how to relate to your 10-year-old, he or she might be 15. In *Once my Child . . . Now my Friend*, Elinor Lenz writes about parents' struggles to let go of their children and how parents can develop new, loving connections with the adults the children have become.

Although many young people say they want to leave home, they also want the emotional and financial security parents provide. They fear the responsibilities of freedom while they hate their dependence on parents. These ambivalent feelings are universal. We can acknowledge ambivalence and empathize with one another in our struggles.

We may not learn how to let our children go or what new insights we can gather by reading about how someone else does it, but knowing others are struggling with similar problems is helpful. Struggling with changing relationships goes beyond a lifetime. Death may end a life, but it does not end a relationship.

For all of us, the family is inescapable. We may worship it or renounce it, accept it or reject it. But we cannot escape from it. We are born into it. It lives with us and through us *beyond the end of our lives*.

## Social Images

The complexity of genetic and environmental factors makes developing a satisfactory self-concept difficult. From perceptions of our physical, mental, social, and emotional selves, we create images. But even when relatively accurate, these images seldom fit into a coherent whole.

The slim, young man may still imagine himself as the chubby 10-year-old he used to be. The beautiful, young model may still see herself as an awkward 14-year-old with braces on her teeth. Confident, young executives may well experience the social anxiety of their adolescent years. These past images have tremendous power over us even when they are no longer valid.

Not only past images but past programming continues to control our lives. Girls are told, "If you behave in a feminine way, some wonderful man will come along and take care of you. And if you are a good girl, you will be rewarded with eternal protection." In *The Cinderella Complex*, Collete Dowling discusses the hidden female fear of independence. In *The Peter Pan Syndrome*, Dan Kiley discusses the male fear of commitment. Thus again, we are faced with human ambivalence—the drive for protection and belonging at war with the desire for independence and freedom.

Although we stress men's and women's liberation, we have difficulty because so much of what we have learned as children sits in unconscious places, controlling our aspirations, feelings, and behavior. Cultural myths, the stories of Cinderella and Snow White, for example, include handsome, brave, young princes who win beautiful princesses. Our hidden fears are that we are the ugly stepsisters or the frogs.

So subtle is our social programming that we rarely know its sources. On the facing pages of a women's magazine, the following advertisements were printed:

- Too fat? X-pills pep-u-up and slim-u-down
- Too skinny? Amazing new X-plan guarantees new curves
- Now . . . whiter, brighter teeth instantly
- Fade out stretch marks. New enriched formula lotion
- Stronger-thicker-longer hair in five days
- Beautiful busts. Money back guarantee
- Natural beauty. Cosmetic face lift. Call toll free
- The hottest new swimwear in nine sexy colors
- Sex—200 explicit photos show you how

Every one of these ads is directed toward our perceiving ourselves as woefully in need of improvement. Whatever we are, we are told we are defective. Television, movies, mass media, and many other forces in our lives are dedicated to making us discontented with ourselves.

---

Before you fall asleep each night, ask yourself

- What did I learn new about myself today?
- What did I notice today that pressures me to conform to images that are not me?
- Did I act as if I expected to solve all of my problems today?
- Did I act as if I expected others to solve all of their problems today?
- Did I act as if my relationships are supposed to be perfect?
- Did I feel as if someone owes it to me to love me totally and unconditionally?

These consciousness-raising questions can help us free ourselves from the tyranny of social values and unrealistic expectations.

Self-concept, then, is the product of how others perceive us, how we perceive ourselves, and how we feel about these images. It is made up of past, present, and future images. It is both personal and social, is constantly shifting, and has no reality except that which each of us gives it.

The social component is made up of such diverse influences as mythology and mass media, a multitude of inconsistent images that we are unceasingly being bombarded with. Yet through the self as we perceive it, we communicate messages to ourselves and others with some degree of consistency and form.

## Multiple Images

The question "Who am I?" like so many questions we ask ourselves, is misleading. It implies I can define and describe myself like a table or chair, that I am some inanimate, unchanging object. It also implies a single self.

William James said, "A man has as many different social selves as there are distinct groups of persons about whose opinion he cares." We range from flexible to inflexible in our willingness to fit our behavior to different relationships and situations. We carry within us the capacity to constantly redefine ourselves. Because we contain the potential for *all* human qualities, we can be warm or cold, dominant or submissive, independent or dependent.

Walt Whitman wrote:

> *Do I contradict myself?*
> *Very well, then, I contradict myself.*
> *(I am large.) I contain multitudes.*

The attempt to create a *single* self in a relationship fosters standardized behavior. We often reward others for their consistencies and punish them for their inconsistencies. We want to be able to predict how others are going to behave. We *expect* them to behave by nonverbalized agreements according to how we define our relationship with them. When another person steps out of a designated role created by unstated expectations, we often experience stress.

Emerson said, "Consistency is the hobgoblin of little minds." Although some human behavior experts say children need a consistent parent, others say a consistent parent does not depict a lifelike model for a child who must function in an inconsistent world. The concepts of consistency and multiple identities can be incorporated into the development of one's self-concept.

Each of us plays many parts in life: child, student, friend, lover, spouse, parent. At times, we play several roles simultaneously. When I walk into the classroom, I put on my teacher hat. When I walk into the house, I wear my mother hat. With my young son, I simultaneously teach, mother, and model what women are like. However, I have little control over whether he sees me as a beneficent teacher or an authoritarian jailer. Sometimes my son and I switch roles. He plays parent to my child. Other times we relate friend to friend.

Although our roles are boundless and always in transition—often with those we love and live with—we get locked in, stereotyped in ways that prevent our genuinely seeing each other. Then, we tend to act as the other person expects.

Every new relationship has the potential for reflecting back to us facets of ourselves that we do not know. The self is mirrored back to us through the perceptions of a new and unique person who sees us as no one has ever seen us before. For those who need consistency, the risk of a new vision of the self is threatening. For others, meeting new people and discovering new facets of the self is a treasure, a delight.

At times, these multiple identities make us feel as if we are unreal. In *Games People Play*, Eric Berne tells us we have three "voices" speaking through us—parent, adult, and child—each accompanied by its own language, body postures, and emotions. The parent can be authoritarian or nurturing; the adult is usually logical and emotionless; and the child can be joyful and fun loving or petulant and rebellious. Those troubled by multiplicity, get into the habit of responding to the world with primarily one role—authoritarian parent or petulant child. A flexible person feels comfortable with a variety of roles and, depending on the situation, can be parent, adult, or child, whichever is most appropriate.

When I fly my small one-engine plane, people often ask if I am afraid. Everytime I get into my plane, the child in me is afraid. But my parent voice says, "Don't be childish," and my adult voice says, "Flying is eight times safer than driving on the freeway." So I get in the plane, sometimes with knees shaking, and fly, which is what makes it exciting.

We have intellectual, emotional, physical, and social selves.

- How do you see your intellectual self? Describe your intellectual strengths and weaknesses. Has your intellectual self-image changed?
- Describe your emotional self-image. Do you cry easily, or do you keep a stiff upper lip? Who told you what emotions were to be expressed? How? When?
- How do you see your body? Describe your physical self. What are your best and worst physical features?
- What makes up your social self? How do you interact in your social world? Close your eyes and imagine yourself in several different social roles acting in ways you normally do not choose to act. What does it feel like?

We have many identities, such as private and public selves. Our multiple selves can be interesting to observe. We can consciously choose that self most appropriate to a particular situation or a unique relationship. We can be controlling, defensive, or cold when the situation or relationship requires, or we can be free, loving, and affectionate.

Practice different selves in your imagination. Imagine yourself as a series of portraits set side by side.

- In the first portrait, imagine yourself sexy, sophisticated, and controlling. How are you dressed? How do you hold your head and body? Listen to how your voice would sound if you were to have a conversation? Now enact a scene in a movie where you play a sexy, sophisticated character.
- In the next portrait, imagine yourself as innocent, naive, and trusting. Dress, act, and talk like an innocent, naive, trusting person.
- Now see yourself as an intellectual professor or drama critic. Next, as a playboy or playgirl. Then, as a housewife or househusband at home with small children.
- Play a series of roles. Create concrete images by imagining a setting, costumes, lighting, and all other props. Act out some different selves.

• Begin to notice each day how you act out different roles with different people: parents, boss, lover, spouse, neighbors.
• Notice what these different selves have in common.

---

The content of your life, like the plot of a movie, has some consistency in the roles that you create. How you act them out may be similar to a B movie, soap opera, tragedy, comedy, or farce. Pretend you are an objective critic, reviewing this movie. How well performed is this play? What does it all mean? What can be learned from observing this character (you) and the patterns of his or her responses and behaviors? By observing your life objectively as an outsider, you may gain some insight into yourself and the patterns of your relationships. Listen to the "voices" in your head that affect your behavior and responses. You have multiple voices: Big Boss, Clinging Vine, Judge, Whiner, Martyr.

Exploring the complexity of our multiple selves is analogous to an iceberg—the tip looks manageable, but below lies an unknown entity. One method of exploration is *internal dialogue.*

---

Write down some names for your multiple voices (for example, optimist/pessimist, independent/dependent, thinking/feeling).

• Make a list of words that fit self 1 and self 2.
• Describe each person.
• Let them have a conversation, and write down what they say.

An internal dialogue among different subpersonalities can result in fusing the best parts into a more unified whole.

---

Separating what I do from who or what I am is unnecessary; they are all connected. My capacity for empathy comes from my multiple personalities. When I am willing to acknowledge all parts of myself as acceptable and lovable, I am less vulnerable to self-deception and self-rejection.

In relationships, we often become attracted to someone who exhibits those parts of ourselves we have rejected. We let them play those roles we do not acknowledge in ourselves. Later, if we marry or live with this other person, we often criticize them for the very qualities we found attractive. Time spent exploring our multiple selves, even those parts in conflict, can help us better understand relationships.

We can never grasp the whole, changing kaleidoscope of the self. Yet at some special moment, we perceive a hazy image, a kind of foundation from which to make decisions about future goals and directions or a way to relate to another person's multiple identities. Human complexity is infinite.

Each of us is perpetually constructing and reconstructing a self-image. It is a role we cannot choose not to play. Creating who we are lasts a lifetime.

Momentary identities ground us and give us a concrete picture like a still photograph. As we look at it and ponder, we know the self is not simply that picture. Selectively, we put the pieces of the puzzle together to see ourselves in the best or worst possible light.

In our search for personal fulfillment, we hope to find the perfect life. The inner journey requiring us to focus on the self takes us through a forest of awareness experiences. However, for those who abandon the road of life and lose their way in the forest of self, commitment to self may replace commitment to others. Exclusively focusing on selfish interests engenders barrenness.

Although exploring intimacy begins with the self, it does not stop there. Now that we have acknowledged how we construct our personal reality from our culture and family, we are ready to explore the discrepancies between fantasy and reality, between who we pretend to be and who we are. Self-intimacy is the bedrock for intimacy with others.

Self-deception is a problem that no one ever wholly escapes. Because the degree to which we can free ourselves from self-deception is essential to self-intimacy, we discuss self-deception in the next chapter.

# Intimacy and Deception    3

> *Deceit is fundamental to animal communication and includes a degree of self-deception through unconscious motives.*
>
> Richard Dawkins

*E* *thics,* the discipline dealing with what is good and bad, offers us a method for creating values to guide our choices and actions. From these values, we judge human behavior, our own and others. Then, we decide who will be the beneficiary—will the action benefit ourselves or others?

We are taught *altruism*—action taken for the benefit of others—is good and *selfishness*—concern with one's own interests—is bad. We are told altruism is superior to selfishness and doing good for others is of greater moral value than doing good for the self. Thus altruism is our cultural ideal.

Research indicates that selfishness or living for one's own welfare is a biological drive. Charles Darwin said that nature's law is one of natural selection in which only the fittest of a species survives. Thus self-survival is instinctive, whereas altruism must be taught for the survival of a society. The survival instinct, then, is the drive to live or survive longer than another person or thing. Faced with a cultural ethic that considers altruism good and an instinct for self-survival bad, many of us try to solve this dilemma through deception.

## The Selfish Gene

Richard Dawkins, in *The Selfish Gene,* says humans are "survival machines," self-seeking and self-replicating by heredity, the genetic transmission of characteristics. Dawkins examines the biology of selfishness and altruism. The dichotomies of love/ hate, fight/cooperate, give/take, generosity/greed are just a few of our ethical conflicts.

Dawkins, a zoologist, says aggression is genetic self-interest. He develops a kinship theory in which a person's investment in the next generation illustrates "survival of the genes." Reproduction to perpetuate the species requires that parents risk themselves for their offspring—for the survival of their genes. According to this theory, survival of an offspring at the possible expense of a parent is a selfish act. Thus genetic selfishness grows stronger as the most selfish persons survive and pass on the "selfish-gene." Survival, Dawkins says, is related to deceit— both deception of others and self-deception.

Dawkins thesis is that as animals, humans are complicated survival machines and are blindly programmed to preserve the selfish molecules, or genes. However, he admits we can teach generosity and altruism to upset our genetic design because inherited traits are modifiable.

Among animals, man is uniquely dominated by culture and learned influences handed down from generation to generation. We teach altruism—actions that enhance others' welfare at one's own expense—which is in conflict with our biological nature. In genetic terms, pure altruism is self-destructive.

To a survival machine, another survival machine (other than one's own child or a close relative) is part of the environment— something that gets in the way. Making the best use of the environment includes making the best use of other survival machines to aid us in the gathering or production of food. Yet as competitors for scarce resources, we tend to hoard and hide as much as we can.

Today, with limited public resources such as energy and water, we hope to appeal to people's conscience—the sense of obligation to do right. We teach a sensitive regard for fairness and justice. When we do not act as we have been taught, we feel guilty. However, psychologists who have studied actual social situations find that individual consciences are not always bound by fairness. During shortages, for example, we see panic buying and gasoline hoarding. Resources available in finite quantities present us with two conflicts: our needs versus others' needs and short-term interests versus long-term interests. People tend to satisfy their immediate needs and sacrifice the future generations' needs.

According to a *Psychology Today* study, most people report

they are concerned about clean air, water, and the environment. They claim to use less than their share of natural resources. Logically, we simply cannot all use less than average quantities of finite, depleting resources. Not trusting others, consumers act out of self-protection. People tend to use resources for their own comfort, profit, or survival. Collectively, individual consumption threatens societal interests. When confronted with these conflicts, many choose the self over the group and short-term benefits over long-term biological preservation.

Biophysicist John Platt calls this dilemma a "social trap." The short-term reward of consuming is more compelling than the long-term reward of not. Our preference for immediate reward reminds us we are members of the animal kingdom subject to Skinner's reinforcement theory.

*Self-deception* creeps in when a person says, "The cost of my using an extra hour of electricity or an extra tank of gas isn't really going to harm anyone." We rationalize that what is beneficial to us will not be detrimental to the community.

Many political economists do not believe environmental or health problems can be solved by cooperation. Considering human nature, they say, we must have rigorous laws and use coercive government powers to control people. Authoritarian governments are based on the belief that people cannot be trusted to act for the common good.

In contrast, democratic governments are based on the belief that the young can be taught civilized behavior, resulting in life at its best. They stress the dignity and worth of the individual, the elimination of discrimination, and equality of opportunity. The ideal is that men and women of good will want a peaceful, prosperous world along with the recognition of common humanity. These governments urge the use of education, reason, and compassion to bring about widespread happiness.

The American Dream is founded on faith in the perfectibility of human beings. This vision makes us seekers who go after possibilities, who can become whatever our visions reveal to us. When we fail to live up to our ideals, we tend to justify and rationalize our behavior. In translating ideals into practice, self-deception helps us bridge the gap.

### Deceiving the Self

William Saroyan says, "Every man is a good man in a bad world—as he himself knows." We tend to think of ourselves as more moral than others. We attribute benevolent behavior to ourselves using the "I" point of view: "I helped that lady in a wheel chair; therefore, I am a helpful person." But inconsiderate behavior we attribute to external factors: "He made a mistake" or "He was wrong." We tend to take credit for positive acts and blame others for negative ones. Generally, our successes we see as products of personal ability and effort, whereas our failures we see as bad luck or the fault of outside forces.

In sports or games, people tend to take credit for winning but find someone or something else to blame for losing. Similarly, students believe a good grade on an exam is a measure of their competence, but a bad grade is the fault of an inept teacher or a poorly constructed, unfair exam. This self-serving bias requires that we put ourselves "one up" by putting others "one down." We generously evaluate ourselves as superior while we evaluate others as inferior. Thus we tend to be defensive—often ready with excuses to protect ourselves.

Psychologists have found that the more people admire a particular trait, such as honesty, the more likely they are to see themselves as more honest than others. We tend to accept and remember more positive than negative information about ourselves. We also tend to consider others less ethical than we are, remembering their mistakes while forgetting our own. Biased assessments of others' character traits, like sympathy, responsibility, and considerateness, occur because our assessments of ourselves are so difficult to measure.

We also like to think we can predict the future. When something happens, for example, who wins (a team or political candidate) or how historical events turn out, we tend not to feel surprised. For other events, we claim "we knew it all along."

For self-preservation, animals in the wild often deceive one another when looking for food. Therefore, deception may be a genetically programmed survival mechanism. Much research suggests self-deception may be a trait bred into us through natural selection.

Thinking positively about our own abilities and traits can provide us with the self-confidence needed to succeed. Thus an egocentric bias, like a self-fulfilling prophecy, can have positive results. Wanting to see myself as honest, when I find someone's purse, I return it. I act out my belief in the virtue of honesty. However, if I fail to return the purse, I either rationalize keeping the money or decide honesty is not such an exalted virtue especially in an unjust world where so many others are dishonest.

We lie to ourselves so that we can believe we have the highest motives while we are actually being self-serving.

Members of successful groups claim more responsibility for their success than members of failing groups do for their failure. When the results are productive, most people regard themselves as having contributed more to the group than others. This self-deception may cause conflict within the work group if individual members expect extra pay or benefits when their organization does well. Yet these same members hardly expect to be docked pay or benefits when the organization does badly.

The social ideal of altruism contributes to both deliberate deception and self-deception. We say, "I didn't tell you because I didn't want to hurt you." Although we prefer to think, "I didn't tell because I am a kind person," we actually lie to protect ourselves, to conceal petty self-interest. We want others to like and admire us, so we try to create impressions that we are good and have the highest motives. When we violate our stated ideals, we tend to conceal the violation from ourselves. In a world without certainty, we often *work* to make ourselves right. Justifying and rationalizing are culturally taught ways to excuse ourselves when we feel we have not met our own expectations.

---

Recognizing that self-deception is a universal human trait can help you avoid judging yourself or feeling guilty as you explore the following:

- Recall a time when you tended to take credit for being helpful, for winning, or for succeeding at something.
- Recall a time when you made someone else wrong so that you could be right or win. Dominating, avoiding, criticizing, or using silence are often attempts to win.
- Recall a time when you put another person down so that you could be one up.
- Recall a time when you justified your behavior or rationalized an action to excuse yourself for what you did.
- Listen for the words *why* and *because*, which often precede a rationalization or justification.

---

*Everyone of us has a potential for violence, a capacity for brutality, a latent sadism.* Unwilling to acknowledge these qualities in ourselves, we project them onto others and find in others a focus for vengeance. We want to destroy any person or group that acts out our own forbidden agendas.

We observe these aspects of ourselves on television and in movies. We avidly read about brutality in the daily newspaper. Curiosity partly accounts for the large audience that TV violence and the mass readership that sensationalism command. We are at once fascinated and horrified by those repressed aspects of ourselves.

Of course thinking about something forbidden is not the same as doing it. Yet most of us avoid admitting even to ourselves that we feel or think wicked things. We want to believe only "bad" people have unacceptable feelings and thoughts. We make a distinction between our own lies and everyone else's. They lie because they are dishonest, evil, weak, or bad. We lie because we are tactful, sensitive, and do not want to hurt others. When we justify our lies to ourselves, we begin to lose the awareness of our lying. As we hide parts of ourselves from ourselves, we lose consciousness of who we are. Polite lies that conceal our badness go underground only to reemerge years later as rebellion and hostility.

Gregory Bateson says the "double-bind" lie occurs when we say "I love you" to someone when unconsciously we also resent them. Logic tells us we cannot experience opposite emotions at the same time for the same person, so we bury ambivalence inside ourselves where it festers.

This discrepancy between our ideal selves and our real selves is often experienced as guilt—an uneasy feeling of pretending to be something we are not. Although we may not act out our cruel or vengeful thoughts, we are so afraid of them that we block them out. Eric Hoffer said, "We run fastest and farthest when we run from ourselves."

At times, each of us will be naive, insensitive, and absorbed in our own kinds of self-deception. The gap between our ideals and our personal progress may cause us disappointment and distress. Yet self-acceptance is crucial to personal satisfaction in intimate relationships with ourselves and others.

Some degree of selfish altruism can bridge the gap between our genetic selfishness and our cultural altruism. Ultimately, honest self-acceptance of both our positive and negative qualities can lead us to self-knowledge and intimacy. By recognizing and respecting our own limitations, we can become wiser and find more satisfaction in our lives.

## Deceiving Others

We first begin to lie as children in *unequal* relationships with parents and other adults who have power over us. We come in conflict with laws and rules that often do not make sense and, for the most part, seem unfair. Lies are most often told when a discrepancy in power exists between two persons.

The people we lie to, particularly those who love us, either consciously or unconsciously pretend to believe our lies. They want to deny what they know. This deception builds an intricate system of barriers to intimacy. Our bodies stiffen against the recognition of lies and in defense of each other.

Parents, who are supposed to be models of virtue—honest, sincere, and good—sometimes lie. "Do as I say not as I do" creates body stress, fatigue, and depression. In hierarchy–power relationships—whether child/parent, student/teacher, or employee/employer—we lie and then resent the person to whom we told the lie. In peer relationships, we lie to gain approval and respect. In intimate relationships, we lie to be loved.

According to a survey in which *Psychology Today* received more than 24,000 responses to a moral and ethical questionnaire, most people do not consider deceiving institutions as serious a moral issue as deceiving spouses, family members, or friends.

In this survey, 45 percent of the *married* respondents admit to having had extramarital sexual intercourse. Of this group, 84 percent feel guilty about their infidelities. Of those married who remained faithful, 17 percent say they would or probably would have an affair if they had the chance. Using answers from *all* respondents, 68 percent think it unethical to cheat on a spouse, but 42 percent of them say they would probably do it if they were sure they would not get caught.

After sexual conflicts, dishonesty with family and friends causes the most guilt. The very things we value so much ourselves, like honesty and trust, are the things we have difficulty giving to others. Thirty-three percent of the respondents say they had deceived a best friend about something important in the last year. Of this group, 96 percent felt guilty about it. We value honesty above many other desirable qualities, but 88 percent of the respondents say they had told little white lies to friends in the past year.

Although more respondents had cheated on their marriage partners than on their tax returns, to save money, 38 percent of the respondents said they either lied or withheld information or tax returns in the last five years. Whereas 84 percent felt guilty about cheating on their spouse, only 59 percent felt guilty about cheating on their income tax. The IRS reported 69 percent of those audited in 1980 owed money and an estimated 20 percent of total U.S. income goes unreported. Many people say they would have no reservations about cheating the IRS if they thought they could get away with it. They rationalize that they work hard for their money, others cheat, and the government spends taxes in unacceptable ways.

A new study in Massachusetts on welfare fraud matched welfare recipients' social security numbers with their bank accounts and found many recipients had in their accounts more than the amount permitted to be eligible for welfare. The state's secretary for human services claims if the pattern of unqualified recipients holds true for the nation, almost $7 billion has been paid over the last five years to welfare recipients who lied about savings.

In the business world, 68 percent of the respondents admit they had taken office supplies or other materials from work in the past year; 47 percent say they had taken sick days when well enough to work; 37 percent say they made long-distance calls at work; and 28 percent say they had cheated on expense accounts.

Workers justify using phones or Xerox machines or padding expense accounts by saying they work overtime and spend their own money and use their own cars for work-related business. Others who conceal a part-time job while collecting welfare or unemployment insurance claim, "Everybody does it."

Two experts, a psychologist and an accountant, report in a study of inventory shortages in department stores (estimated at $16 million a day) that 10 percent is due to error, 30 percent to shoplifting, and 60 percent to employee theft.

Many of us avoid disagreeable realities by ignoring them. Repression—the deliberate exclusion from consciousness of an idea, desire, feeling, or experience—is a denial of reality. Those who cheat on taxes, welfare, unemployment insurance, and other social welfare programs tell themselves they are cheating the government. They repress that they are actually stealing from the paychecks of tax-paying workers: their neighbors, relatives, and friends.

At times, many of us feel powerless. Our lives seem to be under the control of large institutions who give us little freedom of choice. In educational settings, 67 percent of students say they have cheated on exams or school assignments. Often, they rationalize this behavior by saying they are forced to cheat by a system where grades open or close doors to their future.

So complex are human motivations that it is difficult to find a source for them. Cheating, stealing, and lying may be partly motivated by revenge—wanting to get back at those in power. But risk and adventure—the thrill of breaking the rules and getting away with it and of doing forbidden things—also often play a part.

Although we have the power and control, we often have difficulty accepting responsibility for our personal relationships. We would like to see ourselves as loving and kind, honest and truthful. Our inborn capacity for cruelty; indifference; thoughtlessness; infidelity; dishonorable acts; betrayals of trust, of friendship, and of love cause us great emotional stress. When our behavior does not match our ethical ideals, we suffer a crisis in self-image. Many of us deal with self-image problems through self-deception.

## Attitudes toward Ethical Choice

To make generalizations about moral behavior is difficult. Little consensus exists about what is right and what is wrong. *Absolutists* set moral rules then demand everyone stick to them regardless of the situation. Their attitude is that what is good and right is good and right in all situations for all people. *Relativists* see little virtue in blindly following rules. They believe we must be flexible, consider behavior relative to the situation and person, and consider extenuating circumstances.

Each of us chooses an attitude—pessimistic, realistic, or optimistic—toward morality. The pessimist says humans are basically evil and motivated by destructive acts. The pessimist adopts suspicion as an attitude toward people's disguised hostilities.

The realist says it seems unwise to have faith in an honor system or to trust others without question. In a competitive society like ours, many people have too much at stake—degrees, financial success, getting ahead, social approval—not to take advantage of opportunities. The realist takes the attitude that people are neither good nor bad; they are human.

The optimist says humans are basically good. Reversing all the statistics in the *Psychology Today* survey, the optimist finds that 8l percent of people always stand in line taking their turn, 68 percent are totally honest with their best friends, 55 percent have not had affairs, 72 percent do not cheat on expense accounts, 63 percent do not use work phones for long-distance calls, 52 percent have not taken off sick from work without being sick, 62 percent have not cheated on tax returns in the past five years, and few respondents cheat or lie habitually. Therefore, the optimist concludes most people are more altruistic than selfish.

---

Your general view of the world—optimistic, realistic, or pessimistic—affects your evaluation of yourself and others. Although one view is no better than another, being aware of how you tend to view life can move you toward less self-deception.

- Would you describe yourself as generally responding to life as an optimist, a pessimist, or a realist?
- Each view has advantages and disadvantages. What do you gain by choosing to be an optimist? A pessimist? A realist?
- Does your view tend to change depending on the situation you are in or persons you are with? (Often we become more pessimistic with an optimist and more optimistic with a pessimist.)

---

Regardless of our world view, we tend to disguise from ourselves feelings of hostility that serve our needs for aggressive action. Hostility does not have an accepted place in modern life. As children, we are taught hostility is a dangerous emotion. Not knowing how to cope with hostility, since it is "evil," we deny our hostile feelings then feel guilty about the deception. Guilt is a highly effective system of social control. Society breeds guilt into us when we are young, and we never entirely stop feeling it. However, we often tend to camouflage our guilt with anger and resentment.

Besides self-deception and deceiving others, still another level of deception occurs in public and private institutions. Eisenhower denied Francis Gary Powers was spying when his U-2 was shot down over Russia. The Watergate cover-up, the Iran–Contra affair, the CIA, the FBI, governments and corporations in every nation of the world lie, cheat, and steal. Institutions seek profit, power, and self-preservation just as people do.

Most nations use defense mechanisms such as rationalization, repression, projection, and justification. The Japanese Education Ministry recently ordered changes in their new history books—changes in emphasis and wording, in the way they will tell their children about World War II. They are setting a time limit on national guilt. Similarly, young Germans are not willing to be burdened with the guilt over killing the Jews. Official Egyptian guides sometimes say the pyramids were built by "volunteer labor" rather than slaves. In the United States, we debate about whether our early history should be taught as profiles in heroics and courage or with more ambiguity. Over time, we too, have rewritten our history books to reflect all viewpoints. Every culture, every country, struggles with its past.

Nations handle aggression, violence, and guilt by reverting to self-deception to protect their self-image. Every nation is confused about ethical issues. What is morally good or bad has no meaning except in reference to the moral value system of a particular society at a particular time in history.

Deception—whether by self, others, government, or industry—is at least partly motivated by fear, helplessness, or hostility. We live as imperfect human beings in an imperfect world filled with conflict, confusion, ambivalence, and paradox, which each of us can learn to productively deal with. Life is unjust and unfair for all living creatures, but as humans we want to believe we can create a world more just and fair than nature gives us.

## Self-Deception

Since whole nations are confused about morality, it is hardly surprising that individual people are likewise confused. We seem to be hallucinating during the greater part of our lives. Seeing our own self-deception is like trying to see into our own eyes. We create illusions, fantasies, visions, and dialogues that we carry out in our minds like movies on theater screens.

Intellectual conflict and emotional ambivalence often result in forms of self-deception. Resistance, unconscious blocks, incomplete cycles, habit prisons, and stock responses are all obstacles to growth and barriers to self-knowledge. We can evaluate these theories of self-deception through our own experiences, but we must guard against an initial tendency to reject certain conclusions because they are uncomfortable or foreign to us.

---

For one week, keep a "defensiveness" diary. Write down the times you felt defensive and the times someone else was being defensive with you. For each entry, ask yourself the following:

- Was some judgment made?
- Was there an attempt to control or manipulate?
- Were there hidden motives?
- Was there an attitude of superiority or dogmatic certainty?

---

To live a life without self-deception is a goal that can never be attained. Self-deception takes many forms such as perceptual distortions, thought distortions, memory distortions, and meaning distortions. Our very language is self-deceptive.

Through detachment—moving beyond the illusions about self and family; beyond dogmas of religion, race, sex, class, and culture—a few fortunate persons move toward a life of less self-deception. But for those who persist in climbing the Everests of self-knowledge, self-deception becomes another mountain to scale—one without a peak.

### Bad Faith

Jean Paul Sartre, in *Being and Nothingness*, uses the expression *bad faith* as a synonym for self-deception. A person acts in bad faith when he or she lies to the self. With lying in general, the liar intends to deceive and does not hide this intention from the self. But bad faith is not recognized as intentional by the liar. With bad faith, a person is more or less the victim of his or her own lies.

Bad faith is hiding a displeasing truth or representing as true a pleasing untruth. One hides the truth from the self. The deceiver and the deceived are one and the same. Thus the subject deceives the self about the meaning of his or her conduct. Social manifestations of bad faith are seen in prejudice, religion, politics, morals, ethics, and human relations.

All relations with others are based on conflict, which occurs because each person is the center of his or her world. In each person's private world, objects and distances are always experienced in relation to the self.

A person encounters the other as another center of reference. In our relations to others, either we seek in some way to destroy them because they threaten us, or we seek to escape by making the other take responsibility for our existence. Either we try to modify our own subjectivity by making the self an object before the other, or we try to guarantee our own subjectivity by making the other an object.

An example, Sartre says, is the female who pretends not to hear, see, or understand a sexual approach by a male. She admits to being conscious of only his respectful or discreet behavior. Although aware of the desire she inspires, she pretends it does not exist. At the same time, she invites it. She pretends not to notice while she permits herself to enjoy the man's arousal. She neither consents nor resists. She sees herself as a passive object that events can happen to but that she is not responsible for. There is some bad faith on the man's side as well. His choice of ambiguous words is explicitly designed so that he can easily retreat to the position of polite friendship in case he has misjudged the sexual situation.

Other examples of bad faith, according to Sartre, may be found in the impotent male and the frigid female who define themselves in advance as impotent and frigid to prove to themselves that no one can force them to perform or put any demands on them. They pretend to themselves that they are neither in control nor responsible.

According to Sartre, whenever we attempt to define ourselves by saying, "I am . . . ," we are guilty of bad faith. For example, the person who says, "I am a homosexual" is demonstrating bad faith. Performing a homosexual act in the past and being a homosexual in the present and future are different things. No person has a fixed nature. "I am an addict" or "I have no will power" or "I've always been this way" are all attempts to forsake any possibility of change by defining oneself as only one thing, which is self-deception.

Another area Sartre discusses as subject to bad faith is emotions. He says emotions constitute purposive behavior. Being sad means first making oneself sad. Sartre says, "If I made myself sad, it is because I am not sad. . . . The dull look, bowed shoulders, lowered head, and listlessness . . . do I not know," muses Sartre, "that I shall not be able to hold on to it?"

Sadness itself is a conduct. Being sad means making oneself sad. Watching oneself be sad, one is aware of one's sadness.

Sartre says emotions are not things in themselves. A person makes an emotion moment by moment as he or she chooses. With emotions, as with almost everything else, we long for an unattainable absolute. We want to experience a pure emotion, one that is itself and nothing else.

If I suffer, I adopt an attitude of suffering. My posture and facial expressions are designed to express suffering. I work at suffering. Others judge my suffering by its outward appearance. But there is never an all-embracing, pure emotion free of the influence of other feelings.

Sartre would say we suffer from not suffering enough. Humans can never say an emotion sweeps over them and compels them to do certain acts; rather, humans choose the manner and degree to which they will act emotionally. Sartre says our basic tendency and most of our projects are guided by attempts to reach false ideals that can never be achieved.

Thus we are constantly troubled by a feeling of unreality. We try to evade the responsibility for free decisions. Even our choice of emotions is a decision. If I define myself as a deep-feeling person, I give myself permission to cry before an incident occurs that calls for crying. If I say, "I never cry," I define myself as an uncrying person and therefore have chosen to repress tears before an incident occurs.

Finally, Sartre says *sincerity* itself is merely a presentation, a task impossible to achieve. If I decide to be sincere, this constitutes purposive behavior and, as such, is insincere, and thus in bad faith. Man is free to choose his emotions and is therefore responsible for them. Bad faith, then, is evasion—concealing knowledge from the self, fleeing from anxiety, and hiding this anxiety from the self—which is an escape from freedom and an attempt to escape authenticity.

Eric Fromm in *Escape from Freedom* says we do not want the responsibility that goes with free choice. Thus many of us hide from ourselves that no decision is a decision, that inaction is a choice. In our flight, we cannot escape responsibility for how we define ourselves and how we act.

When we violate our stated ideals, we tend to conceal the violation. When the one telling the lie and the one lied to are the same person, we experience confusion and discomfort. The potential for violence, the capacity for brutality and sadism are human qualities we do not want to acknowledge in ourselves.

Secretly, most of us have wished misfortune—sickness, disability, death—befall someone who has hurt us. Perhaps we have wished great tragedy for those in authority—boss, police, government—people who have left us helpless in a system we are powerless to change. Most of us are appalled at our own "evilness," so we project it onto others. Then we become paranoid thinking "they" are out to get us. For self-protection, we want to destroy them before they destroy us.

Self-deception is at the very foundation of the crisis in intimacy. We can acknowledge destructive feelings and thoughts and face them without shame, since they are not actions. Through recognizing both our positive and negative aspects, we can find self-acceptance, which leads to less self-deception.

### Defense Mechanisms

Freud believed to escape pain, frustration, anxiety, or guilt, we developed certain defense mechanisms, most of them unconscious. The word *mechanism* implies something machinelike or automatic that occurs without our awareness. Often, we are unconscious of using defense mechanisms. Sometimes we have partial awareness or a fleeting insight into defensiveness; other times we consciously and deliberately tell an out-and-out lie.

We use defense mechanisms for our own peace of mind or for self-survival. The integrity or worth of the self is constantly endangered. Humor is one way we bring these defenses out into the open; we laugh at ourselves as vulnerable humans. Most of us are far better at recognizing how others use defensive maneuvers than we are at recognizing how we ourselves use them.

---

The following list summarizes some of the ways we escape from reality or defend our self-image. Defensive maneuvers can be sophisticated and difficult to detect. Although defense mechanisms can have positive results, they compound our problems when they are self-defeating.

Although labeling and classifying into lists oversimplifies a complex process, brief definitions and examples can help us recognize habitual, unconscious patterns.

- *Denial*—refusing to admit a threatening reality: A person denies a vision problem to avoid wearing glasses.

- *Projection*—attributing one's own qualities to others: I want sex, so I accuse the other person of being a tease.
- *Rationalization*—giving socially acceptable reasons for behavior: "Everybody does it." "It's for your own good."
- *Displacement*—shifting a thought, feeling, or action from one object to another: My boss criticizes me, so I fight with my spouse, who spanks our child, who kicks the dog.
- *Identification*—establishing a oneness with a valued person, group, or thing and drawing on its qualities: A student who identifies with a famous actor majors in drama.
- *Compensation*—substituting achievement in one area to make up for failure in another: A student excels in football to compensate for a reading handicap.
- *Regression*—reverting to immature behavior: A married partner goes home to a parent after an argument with a spouse.
- *Repression*—automatic inhibition of a threatening stimuli: An older person prefers being seen with younger persons because of fears about aging and death.
- *Reaction-formation*—controlling threatening impulses by emphasizing opposite ones: Wanting to hit someone, an aggressive person touches and hugs others instead.

---

We rely on defensive patterns to cover deep, underlying convictions of our own inadequacies. Feeling inferior, guilty, or worthless, we turn to self-deception for security, confidence, and survival. Disappointment or distrust of the self leads to an inability to develop intimacy.

Like soldiers in a war, we want to survive. But we may use so much energy defending ourselves from imaginary enemies that we cannot cope with real life. Becoming aware of our defenses helps us face unpleasant truths, abide criticism, confront real problems, and accept responsibility for our behavior—even if we suffer pain as the price of giving up self-deception. Although pain often blots out reality, full consciousness can redeem it.

Not all lapses in memory can be attributed to repression or self-defense. Scientists do not know how human memory works. Although some memory theory suggests the brain is like a recorder that registers everything we experience, more recent research indicates there is no tape recorder in the head, no playback to repeat memories. Lawrence C. Kolb, of Columbia University, says sometimes we never register what happens to us, and other times we register only bits and pieces of an event.

For example, questions can change what we remember. In one study of eyewitness testimony, the question was asked, "How fast was the car going when it passed the barn?" People not only remembered the speed but also the barn when, in fact, there was no barn.

Research indicates human memory is fragile and elusive. Our memories are influenced not so much by what we see but by later information, inferences, and other occurrences. Therefore, although defense mechanisms can be useful and are worth examining as possibilities, not all lapses of memory are necessarily repressed or denied information. Often we simply try to tell logical stories.

Ambivalent feelings, contradictory thoughts, interpersonal conflicts, and social confusion exist to enrich our lives. Paradoxes and polarities make up the whole person. If we deny or conceal one part of ourselves through fear, we create imbalance.

Each of us fights daily to restore the lost equilibrium between inner and outer reality. Never static, equilibrium is endlessly changing. Like tightrope walkers, we must make small adjustments, keep a continuous balance to control irreconcilable forces.

Self-approval includes accepting both the hero and the villain in ourselves. When we have both an accurate and acceptable self-image, we are less apt to hunger for others' approval. Through introspection and self-examination, we can enjoy our virtues and admit our defects. The paradox is that when we do *not* seek others' approval, we often get it.

---

Deception in relationships often occurs because of self-deception. This deception has its price: we lose touch with our real selves, and alienation from the self prevents relationships. With awareness, we can move toward less self-deception.

- Recall a time when you wanted someone's approval so much that you distorted your thoughts, feelings, or actions.
- Recall how you justify or rationalize your distortions (for example, "It's not my fault," "I couldn't help it," "I shouldn't feel this way").
- Recall a time when you felt guilty. Guilt can be transformed into disguised hostility, displacement, projection, resentment, or open antagonism.

- One way of eliminating people from your life is by putting them on the defensive. Describe a situation in which you eliminated a person by playing I win, you lose.

---

Hatred and righteous indignation create energy that can be used destructively or constructively. To become autonomous, we must give up hatred and self-deception; accept both positive and negative aspects about ourselves, including those aspects we have rejected; and acknowledge we are both free to choose and responsible for our behavior.

Self-deception and deceiving others may be, as Richard Dawkins tells us, part of being survival machines—making the best use of the environment and other survival machines. Deception is also part of being a member of a society that values the ideal of altruism.

However, we need not give up our visions, our faith in human potential. In *Walden*, Thoreau writes:

> If one advances confidently in the direction of his dreams, and endeavors to live the life which he has imagined, he will meet with a success unexpected. . . . If you have built castles in the air . . . that is where they should be. Now put the foundations under them.

In the next three chapters, we explore our visions of perfectibility through human relationships—how our dreams of love and marriage contribute to the crisis in intimacy.

# Intimacy and Attraction      4

*When you are joyous, look deep into your heart*
*and you shall find it is only that which has*
*given you sorrow that is giving you joy . . . I*
*say unto you, they are inseparable.*

Kahlil Gibran

Having established that intimacy is a choice rather than an instinct, we can explore it for those times in our lives when we opt for closeness. Our original premise is that if we create a context for our lives—a philosophical foundation—from which we do *not* expect others to provide us with satisfaction, we have a better chance of achieving intimacy. We can develop an ability to welcome crisis—danger as well as opportunity—and make a commitment to a lifetime of self-exploration. This continual change requires regular personal and social redefinition.

Which of the following goals is most important to you?

- To discover self-deception
- To incorporate the ideal with reality
- To review how you choose others in relationships
- To acknowledge that intimacy and conflict are inseparable
- To give up the search for safety through relationships

Making a commitment to our goals means, in part, agreeing to accept responsibility for our own lives and acknowledging we must find our own answers and make our own decisions, for there is no *one* best way to live. Each of us is the author of his or her own life.

## Life Is Fiction

The story of your life is fiction. From millions of puzzle pieces, you have culled only a few—those that (for complex and often unknown reasons) you wanted. Then you assembled the pieces into a picture, a self-image. So you not only chose some pieces rather than others, you also arranged them to your liking, in a pattern consistent with your self-concept.

As you put the pieces together, every once in a while, your elbow hits one corner of the picture that you have already created, and you start again. The illusion is that you will one day finish the puzzle and finally know who you are. The reality is that, like a kaleidoscope and unlike a puzzle, you are changing all the time.

Stories have a plot, a theme, characters, and a setting. The setting includes your culture—when and where you were born— and your family—their socioeconomic conditions and the life experiences of each member. Even your family name influences your self-concept. You write your story from your personal viewpoint, for you experience yourself as the main character, the central figure in this drama.

Americans love romance and success stories. Cinderella and Prince Charming *always* live "happily ever after." For a little spice, some of us write a romantic triangle in which sex is the main theme. Stories of self-sacrifice and martyrdom are common. Success stories often begin with a main character born in poverty who struggles in a Horatio Alger fashion or who has a great creative mind that results in some scientific discovery. We dream of fame, money, romance, and sex.

Rich, beautiful, courageous, intelligent, and successful are not enough. As main character, we must also be honest, kind, loving, generous, sensitive, sincere, dependable, and all the other qualities we have been told are good.

Each of us wants to believe we are the hero of something important in the universe. As hero and main character in our story, we need conflict, so we create at least one villain, a powerful antagonist—parent, society, institution (school, government, church), political or corporate establishment—cast as a great adversary interfering with our personal progress.

As hero, we create others in our story for the sole purpose of making us unhappy. Their main mission in existing, as we see it, is to make us miserable. These characters are the bad guys. We work hard, usually through the use of self-deception, to believe we are the good guys.

Many adult stories are of internal conflicts where the hero is torn by indecision, guilt, anxiety, and other burdens that we believe have their origins outside us. In any event, regardless of the plot, let us see how we create the other characters in the stories of our lives.

### The Hero and the Villain

In writing the story of our lives, we pretend we are good. Since villains are bad, we disown the dishonest, undependable, unreliable, unkind, unloving, insincere parts of ourselves and project them onto others around us. When we split ourselves into parts and disown the parts we despise, we cannot learn to love ourselves. Being unwilling to accept these counterparts of ourselves, we pretend they are in others; then we cannot love them either. Until we can be at peace with our whole selves, intimacy in relationships will be but a fleeting fantasy.

Every way of thinking, feeling, and being has its opposite. To know I can be kind is to know I can be unkind. Our language furnishes us with knowledge of our opposing qualities: loving/unloving, powerful/powerless, distant/close, free/unfree. *Ambivalence is the coexistence of opposite feelings about the same person or object.*

We acknowledge the positive aspects of ourselves but not the negative ones that go with them. We feel torn by the struggles between opposing forces. Most of us have little difficulty recognizing when we clash with others, yet many times we are unaware of ambivalent feelings within ourselves. These *intrapersonal* conflicts are not only the most hidden, they are also the most painful. Although we think we must choose one or the other opposing feeling, we can regard them both as true and valid.

Ambivalence is an invitation to self-knowledge. Desiring both independence and dependence, wanting both freedom and closeness, and having concern for both self and others simultaneously are common internal conflicts.

As children, we heard, "*Good* children would never resent their parents considering how much the parents have done for them and how much the parents love them." Still, everyone of us feels or has felt resentment toward our parents for the restrictions they placed on us and the power they had over us. Since only evil children hate their parents and since I sometimes hate my parents, I must be evil.

As adults, we can recognize that we both love and resent the same person; thus we can understand how our children and others who love us also resent us for the restrictions implicit in every relationship.

Besides ambivalent feelings, we also have contradictory beliefs. *A belief is a confidence in an alleged fact without positive proof.* We have inside us belief systems that affect our perceptions. For example, a large college class was divided into two groups. Half the group was told the lecturer was a "very warm person." The other half was told he was a "rather cold person." Together, the two groups went into the lecture hall to hear the man's lecture. After the lecture, those students who *believed* the man was warm rated him more considerate, sociable, and humorous than those who believed he was cold. Of those who believed he was warm, 56 percent participated in class discussion. Of those who believed he was cold, only 32 percent participated.

*Our beliefs affect our perceptions and restrict our choices in life.* A belief system is the organization of everything a person believes. It is composed of all the things we agree with—all the information, biases, and attitudes we have accumulated since birth. We also have a *disbelief* system composed of all the things we disagree with. These two systems affect our openness to information. Research indicates most of us are open to those people who believe as we do, who support and verify our beliefs.

Most of us are close-minded about those things we do not believe. Seldom do we listen to views that contradict our own. In fear, we tend to avoid people whose beliefs differ from ours, which restricts our capacity for intimacy.

### The Love Story

In writing the script for a love story, we create a romance by searching for a *perfect person* to fall in love with. Although we may be unable to define the word *love*, when love hits us, we know it. Here are three descriptions of falling in love:

> I feel like I'm floating on a cloud. I want to run and jump and scream. I have trouble concentrating. I feel giddy. I experience heart palpitations and rapid breathing.

Sometimes I feel on top of the world; other times I am in the very "pits" depending upon the responses of the one I love. Everything I do feels like I'm just marking time, waiting for the moment we can be together again.

I experience physical sensations—cold hands, butterflies in my stomach, tingling spine. I have insomnia. I can't think of anyone else but my lover.

The idealization of love is a very real physical, emotional, mental, and spiritual experience.

---

Besides these experiences of *being in love*, we have certain beliefs about love. Which of these do you believe?

• When you are really in love, you are not attracted to anyone else.
• Falling head over heels in love proves your love is real.
• To be in love with someone without marrying him or her is tragic.
• Having common interests is not important.
• If you are really in love, you will adjust, and differences will disappear.
• Love at first sight is often the deepest, most enduring type of love.
• Marriage without love cannot possibly be a happy state.
• When you are separated from the one you love, your life is empty.
• Somewhere there is an ideal mate for each of us.
• All we have to do is find that perfect person to make our lives perfect.
• Real love comes only once in a lifetime and is eternal.

---

According to recent college surveys, these beliefs about love in the abstract change when young people are actually in loving relationships. Each successive year, from ages 18 to 22, people tend to become more realistic about love. Those engaged to be married are more realistic in their beliefs about marriage than those who are not engaged.

Researchers at the University of Michigan found men usually fall in love first, whereas women remain skeptical or uninterested. Moreover, it is usually the woman who calls off the affair and the man who carries the torch.

These findings fit the biological theories about males and females. Males compete for access to females, and females choose mates that contribute maximally to reproduction. However, once feelings of love are acknowledged, the female is more apt to experience euphoria and to idealize her lover by finding him "not selfish, not moody or quick tempered, not stubborn or irritable." Females further claim, "I could not have a better relationship with another person," a possible rationalization of a choice once made or resolution of cognitive dissonance.

Our beliefs and assumptions about what we "should" feel when we are in love have a profound affect on what we experience, both physically and emotionally. Our bodies respond physiologically to our expectations. Both body and mind shape emotions. Thus we experience a passionate attraction—*an intense state of physiological arousal and emotional absorption in another person, accompanied by a longing for completion and fulfillment.*

The search for completion and fulfillment through another person, for joy and happiness through a relationship, requires that we hide some of our feelings. Hidden beneath affection and tenderness, we often find hostility and envy. We resent those we are attracted to for the power they have to withhold what we want from them. Our anger toward them cloaks the fear that no one can give us what we want—unconditional love, completion, total fulfillment.

True love, we have been told, is unselfish. But usually we love in order to get love. Therefore, both selfish and unselfish love are part of the love experience. Behaviorists believe we are attracted to that which gives us pleasure and repelled by that which gives us pain—whether it be objects, interests, or people.

*Fear* tells us when to avoid psychological danger. Often, expressing itself as suspicion, it prevents our taking unconditional risks. Historically, in some cultures, men owned their wives, as they did their cattle and sheep. We are responsible for the things we own. Today, human beings cannot be possessed, so we fear being abandoned. This fear leads us to exact from our lovers promises of permanence, which are unenforceable.

Loving is inseparable from fear of being abandoned. When we were very small, our mother left us to go shopping. Not knowing she would return, we felt abandoned. Most of us have loved a pet or person who died and left us. As young adults, we leave our families to go out into the world. As we grow older, friends and relatives die. We learn existence is finite, and we must all die. Therefore, *every* relationship ends—either through death or separation.

We learn love is limited and conditional. In most love relationships, one person is more willing to risk closeness than the other; one person is less suspicious or feels the risk is worth the reward. Usually, this person trusts his or her own instincts for survival. Placing one's self completely in the hands of another is dependency—in essence, self-annihilation.

The opposite of love is not hate. The opposite of love is indifference. Since we are all engaged in the crisis of intimacy, we must overcome indifference by giving more love to ourselves, which ultimately will let us give more love to others.

*Love for another person usually begins with attraction.* We can be physically, emotionally, or intellectually attracted to another person. In one research study, people were asked how important physical attractiveness is in choosing a date or a mate when compared with qualities such as sincerity, individuality, dependability, intelligence, personality, and character. Most people ranked physical attractiveness way down the list. Later, at a college computer dance, these same people were given a questionnaire to fill out. When given a choice of future dates, they overwhelming chose the most physically attractive.

Researchers have long questioned the validity of self-report questionnaires. As you read statistics based on this kind of response, in this book as well as in others, be mindful that self-deception—interviewers' and interviewees'—influences research results. Behavior studies often contradict self-evaluations. When we lie to ourselves, we exacerbate the crisis in intimacy.

## Attraction as Fiction

Many young people believe falling in love just happens, as it does in the movies. With experience, we learn love at first sight is more complicated than it appears. To describe being attracted to someone, we use such words as *like, love, fond of, affection for, drawn to,* and *interested in. Attraction for another person is a predisposition to respond favorably toward a particular person.*

Among the variables that lead to attraction is *proximity*—living near or working with another person. The more often two people see each other, the likelier they are to want to spend more time together. Of course we do not choose to be emotionally close to people simply because they live close to us.

We are more attracted to people with similar backgrounds, interests, beliefs, attitudes, values, and behavior. We tend to be more comfortable with people who act, feel, and think as we do—*those who are most like us.* We tend to choose others similar in age, experience, religion, status, education, and socioeconomic level. The word *homogamy* refers to findings that, in general, husbands and wives in American families resemble each other in various physical, psychological, and social characteristics. We feel safest with people like ourselves.

Computer dating companies ask people what they want in a partner—age, habits (smoking, drinking), body structure (height, weight), race, religion, interests, and so on. These services assume people with common interests and values will be most compatible. One research finding is we choose *friends* who are similar, yet we are often attracted to a member of the opposite sex with complementary traits. Although we tend to distrust or fear people who are unconventional—who have values and lifestyles different from ours—we are attracted to them.

---

Most people have a list of qualities they find attractive in the opposite sex.

- What qualities do you find physically attractive?
- What social qualities do you find attractive?
- Are education and background important?
- Is class, race, or religion important?

Write a description of a person you find attractive. With experience, the qualities you seek often become more realistic, though the list often becomes longer.

---

### Complementary Traits

The theory of complementary traits suggests we are attracted to others who have a type of behavior or a set of characteristics opposite our own: An independent person is drawn to a dependent person; a dominant person, to a passive person; a highly emotional person, to a highly logical person. *In a relationship, people are often attracted to others whose qualities they themselves have not fully developed.*

Each of us has the potential to be independent and dependent, dominant and passive, emotional and logical, extroverted and introverted, and all other humanly possible ranges of behavior. Therefore, a person who seeks recognition may be attracted to a person who shows respect and esteem for a superior. These two people find some of their needs met in a relationship based on complementary traits.

When people with complementary traits live together, they often discover their opposite qualities clash. For example, he is a democrat, and she a republican; he enjoys political history, and she romance novels; he likes suspense movies and she "tear-jerkers."

Personal habits can also become irritants. For example, she dislikes his leaving his beard hair in the sink after shaving, and he gets irritated when she takes too long in the tub. She disapproves of the way he wolfs down his food, and he of the way she drops clothes on the floor. He is slow and methodical, and she fast and impulsive. She is efficient and driving, and he passive and relaxed. Or he is decisive and action oriented, and she a thinker or dreamer. He may take 10 minutes in a restaurant to decide what to order, and she 30 seconds. Different decision-making habits and skills make it difficult for opposites to live together. However, in the attraction stage of a relationship, complementary traits that contain the potential for irritation and frustration go unrecognized.

### Filter Models

Some psychologists suggest a filter model to explain the dating and mating process. This theory suggests, of the hundreds of people we meet, only a few get through several different filters. The first filter is *proximity*—people date those who live near them. The second filter is *social homogamy*—similar interests, socioeconomic class, and values. The next filter is *complementary needs*—a submissive person tends to meet the needs of a dominant person. Need-compatibility can be measured by the needs of power and control. Some people like to be led, and some like to lead. Some like to take responsibility and control; others want to be controlled. Two people who both want to lead or control get into power struggles. Since both cannot have their power needs simultaneously satisfied, they tend to be incompatible.

Another filter occurs when two people agree that each will take a distinct *role* in a relationship. When the male's role was clearly defined as breadwinner and the female's as housewife, the compatibility of the relationship rested on each person's adapting to his or her accepted role.

In most relationships, we tend to take roles: male or female, husband or wife, parent or child, buyer or seller, client or therapist, student or teacher. Although the role behaviors may be unconscious, they are clearly defined by actions and mutually agreed on by both persons.

Courtship patterns occur almost ritualistically. Courtship roles provide guidelines for acceptable behavior in initiating relations. Today, many roles have become less defined, more confused, more elusive; still, some roles remain familiar, and we can still identify their patterns.

In *Games People Play*, Eric Berne suggests each of us has certain personality states: parent, adult, and child. "Voices" within us affect our posture, gestures, attitudes, and relationships. In some relationships, the roles taken are those of parent and child. Most of us tend to gravitate toward the familiar. We tend to relive in the present the patterns we established early in our lives. Thus to some degree, we are attracted to others who resemble our mothers or fathers. When someone has had an especially powerful relationship with his or her mother, part of that person wishes to repeat the past. Some men, when they grow up, are attracted to motherly women. She may have been the older sister in the family or rewarded all of her life for being a responsible caretaker. When this kind of man meets that kind of woman, they may think, "This is what I've been looking for," and a romance unfolds based on their playing out these roles.

Often this unconscious recognition results in a mother–son or father–daughter relationship. The woman takes the role of all-sacrificing, nurturing mother, and the man takes the role of the lovable son. Or the man takes the fatherly support role for a woman who wants someone to take responsibility for her life. Although motivations are complex, scripts in relationships are often a replay of the past and last only as long as both parties remain satisfied with their roles.

## Exchange Models

Another theory suggests many people debate whether being married is better than being single. Although marriage offers rewards, it means accepting certain restrictions and responsibilities. Those who decide marriage has more advantages than not must choose one person, from all those they are likely to meet, who they believe will be the best candidate. The person they consider potentially rewarding they pursue. Persons with equivalent resources are most likely to maximize each other's rewards, allowing each to get as much as they can for what they give.

Thus marriageable persons seek out those whom they perceive offer the best opportunities. Some pass up several good candidates waiting for someone better, then sometimes criticize themselves for being too particular.

Some computer dating questionnaires try to match people who have similar "market values"—income, education, social class, age, and physical attractiveness. Today, interpersonal skills, like the ability to communicate, and personal assets, like sensitivity and awareness, have become important in attracting others. Everyone wants, in another, as many socially desirable characteristics as he or she merits or can obtain.

People who find someone of equal attractiveness are in the best "bargaining" position. People do not want to settle for someone less attractive than they. However, when people meet someone who has *more* assets than they have, they, risking rejection, are more likely to pursue him or her. Women often prefer men a few years older than they are because these men are often better established in their work, more dependable, and better providers. One study showed only 1 percent of women prefer a husband to have less education, 18 percent prefer he have the same amount, and 81 percent prefer he have more. However, 82 percent of the men prefer a wife to have the same education.

People in a singles group were asked what they were looking for in a relationship. One young man said,

> A girl who is beautiful, younger than I am, a few inches shorter, same religion and race, equal in intelligence, a virgin, willing to live with me before we get married, a good cook and housekeeper, tolerant of the work I do, sexually desirable, a nonsmoker and moderate drinker. It would be nice if she liked to dance and go to the movies, too.

People who write impossible lists with incompatible qualities, then eliminate others on the basis of these lists often do not want relationships. They just believe they do.

Most people date several others, comparing each person with their ideal. They ask themselves, "Can I do better than this?" They estimate their own desirability by evaluating the desirability of those whom they date. Exactly how they fix these levels depends on their observations of eligible partners and their success or lack of it in attracting others. Ordinarily, people do not proceed toward marriage unless the prospective mate is at or above their own level. This model of *maximum profit* suggests people choose those partners that offer the most advantages in marriage.

The "knight on the white horse" and "beautiful princess" are common fantasy partners. People who continually reject possible partners for their "dream" partner may unconsciously fear intimacy. Although they say they want to be married, searching for the perfect mate probably reveals they unconsciously prefer being single. What we do is often a more accurate indicator of our wants than what we say.

### The Equity Theory

People who seriously want to get married know they cannot have exactly what they want and will settle for those few things they want most; they learn to compromise. They accept that they have to give a little to get a little. Some people hope if they give more, they will get more. Others secretly hope to change the person they marry.

People feel most comfortable when they get, in a relationship, what they feel they deserve. Partners in unequal relationships feel uncomfortable. Those getting less are often resentful, whereas those getting more often feel threatened or guilty and fear they will be left.

The person who benefits most in an unequal relationship sometimes tries to give more attention, loyalty, or freedom to a partner to restore equity in the relationship. An older man may offer financial security to a beautiful, young woman. A plain, overweight woman may give a handsome man warmth, freedom, and fidelity.

A recent study reported in *Psychology Today* tallied 62,000 replies on dating and mating. Readers were asked, "Are you more attractive, slightly more attractive, as attractive, slightly less attractive, or much less attractive than your partner?" Those who rated themselves and their dates as equally attractive also rated their relationships as most comfortable.

Advertising, fashion, entertainment (movies, television, magazines) all teach us what physical attractiveness is. Children, 5 years old and younger, already know what kinds of faces and bodies are considered attractive.

In *The Hite Report on Male Sexuality*, Shere Hite asked 7,239 men, "What things about women, in general, do you admire?" They answered breasts, legs, color of eyes and hair—all physical attributes. In a recent *Esquire* poll, women ranked eyes as a male's sexiest part. However, when the New York *Village Voice* asked a large sample of women what they considered the sexiest part of a man's body, the buttocks and a flat stomach received the most votes.

Still, in several research studies, men and women alike denied the importance of physical attractiveness in choosing a date or mate. When asked, "What are you looking for in a mate?" most people listed qualities such as sincerity, individuality, dependability, intelligence, personality, and character. One man said, "I score women from 1 to 10. I give 9 points to a woman who likes me." Being accepted often outweighs other qualities.

Men and women have always valued personal appearance; the face has been the chief object of attention, judged primarily by others. No one living in solitude, however, would care much about his or her physical appearance.

In relationships, researchers find those less physically attractive sometimes compensate by being richer or better educated, by having professional status or social class. Others compensate for a lack of physical attractiveness by being more loving or self-sacrificing.

Patterns from our relationships with our parents and habits we acquire over the years affect how we are attracted to others. The reason we are attracted to some people and not to others is often learned and founded on illusions we are unwilling to give up. Attraction based on need results in looking for others whom we feel can complete us.

Attraction to others is based, in part, on fantasy and self-deception, which contributes to the crisis in intimacy. When we find completion and fulfillment through a personal quest, independent of attraction to and approval from others, we move from dependency and vulnerability to opportunity and strength.

*We can learn to live with the discrepancy between our ideals and reality without self-deception.* The heroic, ethical, altruistic part of us is the ideal. The self-love, self-interest part of us, which is essential for survival, is the reality.

We need not live in the either-or trap of altruism versus self-interest. The ideal and the real are not necessarily opposites. We can live with an awareness of our fictions. Beyond the initial attraction of a beautiful or handsome face, most of us are drawn to those who have a zest for life and an interest in others. People who are enthusiastic and passionately interested in everything they do, create an attitude toward life that spills over into their relationships.

To some degree attraction must be reciprocal. Thus we wear masks, feign an attractive manner, and play roles. We fear disclosing ourselves as we really are. Self-disclosure makes us vulnerable; it means taking risks and trusting others.

## Trust versus Distrust

We are afraid of being conned. We believe only the vulnerable or uneducated can be swindled. To protect ourselves (the heroes) against them (the villains), we play different roles depending on our self-image. But since we wear masks, we unconsciously fear others are concealing their imperfections too.

Most books and manuals on relationships and marriage devote pages to the subject of trust. *Trust is the assured reliance on something or someone.* We question placing our trust in things outside ourselves. No one can tell us that we should risk unless we carefully weigh the consequences. Trust cannot have value by itself; it is relative to the context in which it occurs.

First comes the question of self-trust. Rarely knowing what we want or how to get it, we fear growth and change. The paradox is that when we do get what we want, most of us set new goals and move on to wanting something new or different. As a result, we find it difficult to trust ourselves.

The more fortunate among us learn to trust their capacities to cope with change, tolerate mistakes, handle pain and vulnerability, be alone or with others, be in a primary relationship or, at times, not have any intimate relationship. Self-trust is a worthy goal, yet we cannot expect to reach some ideal condition and stay there. When yesterday's conditions no longer fit today's, change is imperative.

Trust and self-disclosure are often considered essential to intimacy. *Self-disclosure is the communication of personal or private information to another person.* It involves trust and risk. In our culture, we also value privacy. Thus we face another conflict in values—privacy versus self-disclosure.

Research indicates men are generally less able or willing to reveal themselves. The male bias is that self-disclosure is a weakness, whereas nondisclosure is a wall against intimacy. The fear someone will get inside us and see who we are seems to be an intolerable risk that many prefer not to take. Since most of us do not know what is inside, we are loath to let others find out first. However, if our goal is self-awareness, we can learn about ourselves through trusting others with personal or private information that they can reflect back by telling us how they see and hear us.

An interesting paradox is that the fear of rejection, of being judged or criticized, often has a self-fulfilling result. We get what we expect—rejection. Each of us must set his or her own levels of trust: in which areas (body, feelings, thoughts), with whom, and under what conditions.

*Self-disclosure* is a term usually applied to revealing secrets. However, trust includes many areas. A person who talks freely about sex and is knowledgeable of all sexual techniques may *appear* to be self-disclosing and trusting yet withhold physical affection and be distrustful of the body.

Possessions and money are related to trust. In our culture, discussing personal finances is taboo. To ask people how much money they make, the amount they have in the bank, or their net worth is considered impolite. Many of us know of hidden bank accounts or assets held secretly by one member of a marriage. Some of the stories about financial manipulations that surface when couples divorce make the unthinking, trusting person appear financially gullible.

Safety and risk, trust and distrust, self-disclosure and non-disclosure are dualities of the same experience. Self-disclosure may enhance a relationship, but it is not guaranteed to do so. Although self-disclosure usually begets self-disclosure, many relationships can be one-sided in intimacy, disclosure, or trust.

A few years ago, experts suggested that "telling it like it is" and "speaking out" are essential to honest, vital relationships. Regrettably, disclosures have often led to hurt feelings and ruined relationships. Although repressing unpleasant thoughts about each other interferes with constructive communication, we can choose, by weighing the consequences of our choices, whether to tell all of it, part of it, or none of it.

In a confrontation, one divorced couple began shouting at each other. She said, "I never loved you." He screamed back, "I never had a happy day the whole time we were together." Later, each admitted to a divorce counselor they indeed had loved each other and they did have some happy times together. But each left the other believing the lies.

Honesty is a fine policy, but we do not always know what the truth is. Disclosure is not a panacea for every problem nor even an end in itself. It can be useful and freeing under some circumstances and damaging and frightful under others.

Theoretically, the more I disclose myself to you the more likely you are to disclose yourself to me. When appropriate and mutually shared, self-disclosure can improve a relationship for a time. The danger is that once you decide what I am like, based on what I disclose, you may lock me into that picture. You will continue to see me as the person I disclosed rather than the person I am becoming.

One of the advantages of self-disclosure is we find others who are similar to us—people searching for the same kinds of fulfillment, suffering the same kinds of pain, experiencing the same kinds of joy. We find most of our secrets are similar and feel united in our likenesses. This confirmation is more valuable at certain stages of our lives than at others. Generally, as people mature, their need for this kind of affiliation and identification becomes less important.

Persons who value loneliness, who feel unique and different, may choose not to acknowledge the ways in which they are like others. They tend to concentrate on the ways in which they differ. Loneliness is not a constant emotion throughout life. A Harris poll found that among adolescents 61.3 percent of the girls and 46.5 percent of the boys said they were lonely, whereas only 13 percent of people over 65 said loneliness was a serious problem.

Besides age differences, women report feeling lonely far more often than men. Yet loneliness is not simply a matter of being without companionship; it is also a feeling of being unconnected or isolated. You can feel lonely in a crowd, at a party, or with someone you love. For some persons, self-disclosure and trust alleviate loneliness.

Generally, women score higher than men in desiring self-disclosure. A person who wants to give and receive self-disclosure may have trouble understanding a person who values privacy or finds more satisfaction in work than in people. In this loneliness survey, people who work reported feeling less lonely than people who do not work.

How much time and energy a person is willing to spend on self-disclosure, trust, and intimacy will be affected by how much satisfaction he or she finds in other areas of life. Since intimacy is often defined as being close, professionals and others who value intimacy tend to think the nondisclosing, distrusting person misguided, which further injures intimacy.

Voltaire said, "The secret of being a bore is to tell everything." When to open the door and when to keep it closed depend on the time, situation, and need-satisfactions of those involved.

Some people enjoy talking about themselves. In listening to others, they may or may not be interested. When they want to learn about others, self-disclosure becomes an invitation, a modeling of something to give and receive. Often those who enjoy intimacy can reach a depth of understanding in a short time. The greater reward, though, may be self-understanding. If you trust and disclose purely to get back what you give, you may be doomed to disappointment.

Trust and risk taking are more attractive choices with a supportive, nonjudgmental person, or when there is a mutual agreement to confirm each other. With strangers, unquestioned trust can be foolhardy.

---

The following elements make trust through self-disclosure risky:

- We may find out things about ourselves we are not ready to acknowledge.
- We risk criticism, judgment, and rejection by self and others.
- We risk having our values, feelings, and thoughts changed when we listen to others whose values and ideas are different.
- If we ask others to trust us, we must be trustworthy.
- If we expect others to be trustworthy and they are not, we may suffer a loss of self-esteem or experience pain.

Where do you fit on this risk-safety scale?

High risk _____ Need for safety

Where do you fit on this self-disclosure scale?

Open _____ Closed

Where do you fit on this trust-distrust scale?

Trusting _____ Distrusting

Our ability to trust others and risk self-disclosure changes as the situations and people change.

---

Whether we are trusting or distrusting, self-disclosing or nondisclosing, to insist that others do as we do or value what we value is unrealistic. We cannot say risk takers are better, more courageous, or more foolhardy than others. Choosing trust and risk over safety is a personal choice.

The more we are able to listen to others and understand what they say as telling us about themselves, the less we need to agree or disagree, believe or disbelieve. Beliefs are not concrete objects with unalterable structures like a ball or a book. No one can steal our beliefs. Whatever we hear that we disagree with, we can set aside like a hot brick until it cools. Later, we can pick it up again and examine it. Although we must make decisions to act, we can keep an open mind to new information.

Such issues as belief in a god, extrasensory perception, astrology, or life after death can be everlastingly debated. Few beliefs are ever completely discredited. A Christian and an atheist argue endlessly about religion. Though their argument appears to be with each other, it is more often internal. Each is questioning his or her own beliefs. One's attack on the other is an attempt to expurgate a facet of the self. This attempt to submerge a part of the self, to alienate and disown or discredit a part of the self, results in a futile, internal, endless conflict.

Ambivalence and conflict are a part of life. We want independence while we want a faithful lover. We want the support of our family while we do not want any demands made on us. We want to be connected to something larger than ourselves—a family and community—while we do not want any rules or limitations placed on our individuality.

These opposites war within us. At times, we may subordinate one to the other. Much of the time, we handle ambivalence and conflict through self-deception. We enjoy romantic stories even though they include elements of deception. We often find fantasy more beautiful than reality.

On this foundation and understanding of the connections between intimacy and attraction, we are now ready to explore the connections between intimacy and love—the different meanings of the word *love*, how love develops, and the different ways we express love.

# Intimacy and Love     5

*'Tis better to have loved and lost,*
*Than never to have loved at all.*
                                    *Tennyson*

F ew topics have such enduring fascination as the nature and
    meaning of love. Every generation seems to produce new
definitions and analyses as well as new literature, art, and
popular music evoking images and symbols of love. Most Americans *believe* in love. Love as a belief system helps us find meaning in life. The modern religion of love portrays love and a
loving relationship as the road to a good life.

The Greeks spoke of three kinds of love: eros, philia, and
agape. *Eros* was personal, emotional, passionate love. Today,
eros is often likened to erotic or sexual love, sometimes viewed
as superficial, selfish, or carnal love. *Philia* was brotherly or
sisterly love—platonic friendship, nonsexual affection, and
caring; today, sometimes called companionate love. *Agape* was
unselfish, transcendental love. It was the ideal—a spiritual or
cosmic, nonexclusive, all-embracing love, a mystical experience
of oneness with all life.

Many books have been written on the subject of love, yet love
remains a mystery that defies understanding. Even though we
may be unable to say precisely what we mean by love, each of us
has experienced either loving or being loved. A child says, "I love
you, mommy" when he means "I need you." A mother says, "I
love you" when she is asking, "Please love me." A father says, "I
love you" when he means "I want you to do what I say." A lover
says, "I love you" when he means "I want to possess you." Our
desires to possess, control, manipulate, and be believed in are
mixed with the concept of love.

The word *love* has no fixed meaning. Love is neither static nor absolute. Each of us uses the word to describe different experiences at different times with different people.

---

- List several ways you use the word *love.* Include loving people, things, and experiences.
- List ways other people use the word *love.* Do you like or dislike how others use the word?

---

Sometimes we experience love as a feeling, an all-consuming, seemingly uncontrollable emotion. Sometimes we experience love as an action like cooking a special meal or buying flowers or a gift for another person. Nurturing love is acting to sustain life and growth of another. Sometimes we experience love as a body response with rocking, hugging, and kissing. Other times we express our love verbally with expressions like "I love you."

Many of us fall into the trap of identifying one kind of love as "true" love, disparaging other kinds as superficial. Many of us long for an ideal, unconditional love—to be loved for ourselves, for who we are, without any expectations or demands. The complication arises when we fail to give this kind of love. We then experience ourselves as unloving, unable to love without anticipation of return.

Love, in Western cultures, is often an exchange of something for something else such as self-identity and security, either emotional or financial. Theodore Reik says love is a reaction formation—a cycle of envy, hostility, and possessiveness. These discrepancies between ideal and real love cause us confusion, discomfort, or pain.

Psychologist Abraham Maslow wrote about two forms of love: D-Love represents *deficiencies* or needs, as in the complementary types of attraction we discussed earlier, and B-Love represents *being,* which recognizes personhood and individuality. D-Love often leads to possessiveness, clinging, disappointment, or resentment when needs are not met. In B-Love, a person is appreciated simply for being the way he or she is. Ideally, B-Love would be love without possessiveness, demands, or expectations. We would not expect anything in return but simply love persons for themselves, both their positive and negative qualities. Such an ideal love is rarely experienced for more than brief moments.

Today, we are caught in a crossfire between the traditional love with lifelong commitment and the more modern love with personal liberation. We search for innovative ways to reconcile deep-seated values: commitment and permanence with freedom and choice.

The language we use to describe our love relationships ensnares us. We want love to be spontaneous, yet commitment means obligation and sacrifice. When we experience moments of not wanting to be together, obligation to the relationship jeopardizes self-interest. Still, love is genuine only when freely chosen. This stress of spontaneous choice conflicts with the sense of love as a duty, as a valid moral commitment. The individuality love affirms remains in tension with the social interdependence it generates.

Most of us question our ability to love and be loved. Do I love him or her enough? Does he or she love me enough? We have been told a meaningful, satisfying relationship with another person is the best road to happiness. Yet we know love is unreliable. We not only cannot depend on love, we cannot even say what we mean by it.

We like to believe someone can love us even when we are ugly inside or out; when we express unacceptable feelings; when we are selfish, impatient, and childish. No matter how we act, we dream of being loved forever by some wonderful person who *never* will leave us.

Many of us want to be the center of another's world—even his or her very reason for existence. In our great love fantasy, like Romeo and Juliet, we would be willing to give our lives out of love for each other.

We believe loving someone makes us more noble, more virtuous. We believe it brings out the finest side of our character. We want to believe if we truly fall in love, our own selfishness would miraculously disappear; we would find ourselves faithful, honest, selfless, and devoted; we would express love creatively and spontaneously; we would communicate worth, dignity, and value to the loved one, who would accept us totally and give us the same.

We have difficulty seeing someone as a hero unless he or she loves someone. The belief in love as a cultural symbol of personal worth goes far beyond the practical needs to marry or have a family. Our belief in love is like a religion, a form of salvation that has the power to bring us happiness.

## Romantic Love

Using established measures of romantic love, a Western Illinois University study of dating students at the college concluded there is but one type of *romantic* love. It involves intense emotional attraction. The concept of romantic love is part of a belief system. Those who believe love is a mad, passionate experience are more apt to "fall" in love.

Experts tell us those euphoric, grand feelings that accompany romantic love are like self-hypnotic dreams; they are unreal. Still, at the moment a person experiences them, they are both real and wonderful. Most of us look back with nostalgia to our romantic love experiences like stars in the heavens of our lives.

Though few of us really believe in the stereotype of love, we want to believe in it. Thus despite knowing romantic love is unreal, we experience it as if it were real. Some people call themselves incurable romantics. The experience of romantic love is so compelling and memorable—even the high point of a person's existence—that the rational thought of romantic love as unreal does little to dispel the experience. Many of us are in love with love.

Dr. Murray Banks says too many of us confuse love with infatuation, which is like confusing a diamond with a zircon. The expressions, "I'm head over heels in love" and "It's love at first sight" are examples, he says, of infatuation. Banks defines love as "an attitude between two people who have enough things in common—tastes, interests, ideals, standards, values—shared in companionship, to make them stronger together than either is alone."

Although a definition like this tries to convince us romantic love is superficial, few of us would forsake the experience. In our youth, we believe one person is exactly right for us. All we have to do is wait for him or her to come along. Common sense tells us this is childish wishful thinking, but it does not change the yearning. The experience of romantic love expresses itself as utter surrender, almost self-abandonment.

Most of us who have had such an experience cherish it and feel sorry for those rationalists who use words like *infatuation* to tell us romantic love is superficial. A few of us become incurable romantics, preferring romantic love to a more permanent, committed love that loses its passion and intensity.

A belief in the power of love to transform us is part of our cultural programming. However, in the languages of some cultures, the word *love* does not exist; therefore, love as we know it is not a universal concept.

Since Americans believe love is supremely important to human existence, we cannot envision a life without love. At the same time, we question the authenticity of love in our own lives and are troubled because we know romantic love is unreliable and nonpermanent. Despite knowing romantic love is ephemeral, we risk the pain for the ecstasy and aliveness of an all-consuming, overwhelming passion.

One of our greatest fears is that we cannot love enough, that we will fail the real tests of love, that we somehow lack the capacity to care enough to set aside our own welfare for the welfare of a loved one. Fearing we cannot love enough, we suspect no one can love us the way we want to be loved. Yet our yearning for unconditional love often perseveres even after our intellect tells us it is unachievable.

Incompleteness in the self cannot be made complete by having someone love us. Men and women who seek validation and fulfillment through another seldom find what they are searching for. Feelings of romantic love are undependable because they are constantly changing, ebbing and flowing. They seem to transform us, for the moment, then leave us with a desperate longing for them. We experienced glorious, ecstatic feelings, which we crave again and again. One man, advertising in a newsletter for single people, writes

> I have known the ecstasy of intimacy where the deepest levels of being are fully shared, where powerful nurturing splits one open to joyous trusting tears. I need a woman to return there with me. It's my deepest essence that I'll share with you if you'll hear my plea and come with me.

The inability to sustain these passionate feelings does not end the longing. So powerful is being in love with love that the fantasy of love is more beautiful than the reality of it.

Romantic love often helps us feel more valuable. But this search to be nurtured and loved, worshiped and adored can result in disappointment or blame of self or partner. Novelist

Somerset Maugham says, "I learnt . . . that love was only the dirty trick nature played on us to achieve the continuation of the species."

How much of the love drive comes from cultural expectations and how much from biological forces cannot be apportioned. Sex and biological drives, as related to love, we discuss in Chapter 7. Efforts to reduce human behavior such as love to some group of explanatory factors is called reductionism. These explanations are usually oversimplifications. However, in certain love experiences, each of us is like all others, some others, and no other. Over time, the longing for perfect love often dissipates as it is replaced by self-esteem, wisdom, and experience.

## Love as Attachment

One definition of love is a "strong liking; fondness and a feeling of strong personal attachment." Some relationships are tied together by affection and contentment along with a joint commercial venture in which partners agree to create a better life, in part, through attaining certain possessions—a house, cars, and so forth.

Lasting relationships usually involve being realistic and knowing what matters most. Two social scientists report the types of belongings people seem most attached to are furniture, art, photographs, books, stereos, and musical instruments. In most instances, these objects are so valued because they are linked to a person, place, or fondly remembered experience.

Men often associate possessions with physical action; they think of sports equipment, cars. Women generally think of objects that allow for contemplation—photographs, artwork, plants. People who are attached to things, according to a team of psychologists, seem to be more attached to people.

These researchers maintain that people who deny meaning to objects are more likely to lack a close network of human relationships. Thus people who say they love objects also say they love people. Perhaps one kind of attachment leads to another—whether possessions, activities, achievement, or people.

Besides saying we love certain objects, we also love certain activities. One man might say, "I love golf," whereas another may give up many things to sit in front of a television set to watch football. Many wives feel shut out by a man's interests.

They say, "He loves that damned football more than he loves me." Traditionally, in our culture, boys grow up having material and occupational loves, and girls, human and domestic ones.

Those who want to idealize love, resent defining it as attachment. Others claim, in our capitalistic Western culture, that love is extremely rare, that persons are often used as need-satisfying objects, for status or role relations, or as an approving or disapproving audience. Similarly, Freud suggests almost every intimate personal relation contains sentiments of aversion and hostility, and we use one another as objects that administer pleasure or pain.

When two things are attached, they are bound together. Two people joined by common interests are linked by common desires. These interests or desires forge bonds of attachment. Thus human life includes bonding to persons, objects, or activities.

As babies, we learn we are given love when we are good, and it is taken away when we are bad. Thus we know love is unreliable. Each of us wants as much love as we can get. Like a bank account, perhaps if we get enough of it, we can put it away until we need it and want to draw on it. But we soon learn love cannot be saved.

There are no guarantees. We cannot weigh love; it does not come in amounts; it is intangible and undependable. Someone who says, "I love you" probably means it for the moment, but love does not shield us from that person's anger, hostility, or disapproval tomorrow. Some people say love is an action, not simply a feeling. If we truly love someone, we would permit them to be free. The paradox of love, they say, is that love is a letting go.

## We Love Many Things

We love many things—people, places, possessions, activities. Many of these coexist. We may love our children, as well as our town, house, work, self, and life.

Usually our many loves nourish us, but sometimes they conflict, and sometimes they cause pain. What we are attached to comes from our past. The sources of our love begin when we are born, and these early experiences of love become unconscious habits, fixations, and attachments.

Love is many different things at different times: positive or negative, pleasurable or painful, happy or sad. When one love satisfies a need without interfering with other loves, we experience it as positive, and we feel free to choose it. Often, however, love may satisfy some needs at the expense of others. When love conflicts with the satisfaction of other things we want, we experience love as negative, as costing more than it is worth. We may experience its negative qualities when love requires time, energy, attention, and commitment.

It takes most of us a long time to discover the only love we can count on is self-love. If we do not learn self-love, we find it difficult to love anyone or anything else. Self-love is the foundation for, and is essential to, all other love. Yet even self-love ebbs and flows with the tides of life.

Self-love includes a love of solitude, with its advantage of time to read, study, write, think, and enjoy things like music and art. Solitude includes the joy of living without effort and making no accommodation to others. Thoreau said,

> I love to be alone. I never found the companion that was as companionable as solitude. We are for the most part more lonely when we go abroad among men than when we stay in our chambers.

The freedom of independence and individuality may be more important to those who have sustained a fulfilling relationship over a long period, perhaps in a marriage or after living together with another person.

As children, we were told promises must be kept. "I love you" often implies the promise to love each other forever, "as long as we both shall live." I promise to love you forever in exchange for your promise to love me forever. The problem is we cannot promise feelings. If love fades, we cannot will it.

However, if love is a behavior, we can will ourselves to act out our promises. One theory suggests if we act out our love, we will feel it. The conflict occurs when love of self wars with love of another. The martyr who gives up what is best for the self out of love for another often feels a sense of abandonment or worthlessness. If we are not good for ourselves, we can scarcely be good for others.

Parents teach what they themselves have been taught: Consistency is a virtue; dependability means doing what you say you will do; a promise is a commitment to perform. Thus when an agreement is unfulfilled, children say, "you promised . . . you promised." Some adults echo that sentiment.

*A promise is an expectation.* Every business, labor, or marriage agreement can be changed, amended, or ended legally. Keeping promises can be both destructive and unintelligent. As adults, we know value definitions are neither absolute nor unalterable. Honesty may be *the best policy*, but it can also be cruel, vindictive, or vengeful.

In *I Never Promised You a Rose Garden*, by Hannah Green, a young girl in a mental institution is afraid to leave. She tells her psychiatrist it is not a fair world out there. Her doctor says,

> I never promised you perfect justice . . . I never promised you peace or happiness. . . . You can be free to fight for all of these things. The only reality . . . is being free to accept it or not at whatever level you are capable. I never promise lies, and the rose-garden of perfection is a lie . . . and a bore too!"

## Love Patterns from the Past

Few people choose mates rationally, according to how many benefits they might offer. Emotional reactions to others are often irrational, unconscious, and complex. Our relationships begin with how we view ourselves as prospects. Who we think we are and how we define ourselves starts so far back in our past that most of us cannot remember how it all began.

For example, 3-year-old John pulls away from his mother and runs off. His mother runs after him, grabs him, and says, "John, you are a bad boy." John then thinks, "Gee that was fun. I like being bad." Once he experiences attention and excitement as part of being bad, he defines himself and continues to behave badly in relationships.

Early in our lives, each of us develops a complex network of preferred ways to behave and respond to others. Then, often unknown to ourselves, we continue these patterns. The wise person will explore his or her childhood to discover as many of these personality patterns as possible.

Although intensity of attachment and affection may be factors of personality, they are also learned. We first learn about attachment to other humans in the context of the family. Our parents and siblings form the core of our first human connections. Then, if as a baby, we are given a teddy bear or rabbit to take to bed, this soft, cuddly animal makes us feel safe. As we get a little older, perhaps we are given a dog or cat we can hold, pet, or talk to. The pet, unlike the stuffed toy, responds to us.

Our capacity for affection begins early, but certain traumas can affect us. For example, when his dog ran into the street and was killed, a 6-year-old boy unconsciously decided he would never love another dog. Some children who have negative experiences with humans unconsciously withhold attachment to others throughout their lives.

Physically abused children often become abusing adults. We learn our physical responses to others at an early age. Most of us hold back to some extent, unwilling to totally risk surrendering ourselves to any other person who has the power to leave us. A common human fear is that we will be abandoned.

Freud suggested all of our attachments have a bodily or physical basis that provides us with sensations of satisfaction and comfort similar to those we felt when we were held as a baby or when we held our teddy bear. Physical satisfaction begins when a wet diaper is removed, when we are hungry and are fed warm milk, when we are afraid and are held and rocked or talked and sung to. Soon feelings of comfort and safety form a pattern of both emotional and physical components. This complex pattern is unique to each person and depends on the nervous system, body structure, family environment, parental influences, and childhood experiences.

### Habit Patterns

A group of research scientists, experimenting with mice, provided the mice with clean cages, the bottoms covered with sand. The researchers put water in containers on top of the sand but buried the mice food about an inch below the surface of the sand. The mice would dig up the food and eat it. After about a month, the researchers put the food in dishes on top of the sand. After eating the food out of the dishes, the mice would dig in the sand. No longer linked to the biological need for food, this sand digging continued.

Although humans dislike thinking they can learn anything about themselves from research with mice, certain habits formed in the first years of life can continue indefinitely. For example, eating is a source of comfort in our first year. Babies often continue to search for comfort through their mouths by sucking their thumbs after they have had enough food for nutrition. Some psychologists theorize that pipe smokers, pencil chewers, compulsive eaters, and fingernail biters are trying to satisfy the safety–comfort needs of those early years. Like the mice that persisted to dig in the sand, many of us persist in old behavior patterns.

Unlike mice, humans can examine their behavior patterns

and trace them to actions and feelings from childhood. Often out of pure habit we continue searching for the comforts, safety, and pleasure of our early years in ways that not only do *not* satisfy us as adults but also restrict our freedom and prevent our finding satisfaction.

Freud called these patterns *fixations*. So disguised do they become that we rarely identify them. Children frightened during a war or by poverty may transfer these fears and insecurities to other symbols, money, for example. After undergoing the Great Depression of the 1930s, some people feel they are safe only if they have enough money.

Sometimes, in relationships, we transfer to others those attachment patterns that comforted us as children. We select with unconscious accuracy a mate who will re-create with us some emotional patterns of our first families.

When, 15 or 20 years later, we find ourselves attracted to a particular kind of person, these connections can seldom be verified, much less identified. For example, little girls with alcoholic fathers may be attracted, as adults, to alcoholic men. If basic biological needs were connected to adults who fulfilled our bodily and emotional experiences as children, we tend to transfer these patterns to future relationships.

If we search and find a relationship based on an earlier pattern of attachment, that pattern becomes reinforced. Freud suggested, in a pattern he labeled the Oedipus complex, boys get attached to certain qualities in their mothers and search for that quality in adult relationships. D.H. Lawrence, in *Sons and Lovers*, wrote of his own attachment to his mother, an attachment that interfered with all of his adult relationships with women. Even after his mother's death, Lawrence was not free.

Originally, Freud's theory applied only to male children and their attachments to the mother. Recent research indicates both sons and daughters search for qualities of their mothers in an adult relationship. A young child accustomed to a parent who screams will likely be comfortable in a relationship with a screaming partner. This could be a compatible, though self-defeating, match if the screaming partner is reinforced for this childish response to strife.

From early childhood, each of us learns models for marriage, femininity, masculinity, motherhood, fatherhood, and other family roles. We blend conscious and unconscious memories and then compulsively repeat and re-create past patterns. These may come from siblings, grandparents, or other relatives with whom we identified. Still, although we are influenced, we are not doomed by our early years. We have the capacity to overcome habits and attitudes developed in childhood. Each of us has hidden strengths and amazing capacities for growth and creative change.

In *Your Inner Child of the Past,* W. H. Missildine contends that adults who have difficulty living full lives and getting along with others are hampered by reaction patterns to parents.

---

Certain parental patterns can produce the following responses in a child. Notice if any of these are familiar to you.

- *Perfectionism* produces preoccupation with accomplishments.
- *Overcoercion* produces dawdling, daydreaming, procrastination, and other forms of resistance.
- *Oversubmission* produces impulsiveness, outbursts of temper, and lack of consideration for the rights of others.
- *Overindulgence* produces boredom, lack of persistence, and difficulty initiating individual effort.
- *Punitiveness* produces fierce desires for revenge that may dominate adult life.
- *Neglect* produces anxiety, loneliness, and difficulty with feeling close to others.
- *Rejection* produces lone-wolf feelings of unacceptance of both self and others.
- *Sexual stimulation* produces emphasis on sex and dissatisfaction with personal relationships.

---

We can sometimes benefit when we explore ways to discover if, as adults, we are still reacting according to past habit patterns so that we can substitute more suitable forms of behavior for those learned as children. The questioning person can test these theories against his or her own experiences.

Until we have completed our relationships with our parents, our whole lives are actually *about* our parents. If we are trying to prove or acknowledge something to them, our lives simply become reaction patterns.

One young woman, reacting against a depressed mother who committed suicide, lives an active life, so full of energy that no one can keep up with her. She lives solely within the top half of the emotional continuum, refusing to let herself become depressed. In coming to terms with her mother's suicide, she realized her life is a rejection of her mother's life. For now, this pattern of aliveness works for her and has become part of her unique identity.

In contrast, sometimes an optimistic parent ends up with a pessimistic adolescent. One father who sees the world through rose-colored glasses tries to convince his son that "life is wonderful, that everything is beautiful." The son responds negatively, as if to say, "Don't tell me how to see the world." The son searches for the negative in reaction to the unreal, rosy parental view. Some of us base our lives on either resistance or acquiescence to parents. As long as we maintain these reaction patterns to parents, we are not free.

When we have worked through our relationships with our parents, we can relate as adults to each new person in an intimate and creative way that is unique to us *as we are today* rather than as we were as children.

### Developmental Love Patterns

Developmental patterns in relationships depend on maturation. As we move from one stage of growth to the next, the patterns of our relationships change. Developmentally, we began with the nurturing mother–baby relationship. Through the age of 5 or 6, we experience an unconditional love from an all-powerful parent who provides us with all of our needs: biological, safety, emotional.

Then from about the ages of 6 to 12, we find peers, other children our age and sex, who have similar interests and will play with us. During this stage, friends are valued for their material and physical assets. A friend is someone who shares his or her bicycle or gives us chocolate-chip cookies. A friend is someone who does what we want.

After the age of 12, in adolescence, we search for collaboration, for mutual support in common interests; we search for someone to share secrets with. Many of us become attracted to someone of the opposite sex and develop romantic attachments. As we search for a way to separate from our parents and leave home, we transfer our feelings of love to someone of the opposite sex. Some adults say they got married so that they could leave home.

Psychologists tell us life cycle stages in interpersonal relationships must be aligned with types or qualities of love experiences.

• The infancy–nurturing period results in the symbiotic love stage.
• The early childhood–parent period develops the affectionate/responsive stage.
• The middle childhood or Oedipal period (boy–mother, girl–father attachments) develops the seductive/possessive stage.
• The late childhood–preadolescent period results in the chum/chum stage of intimacy.
• The youth period results in the lover/lover stage of romantic passion.
• The adult period develops the mutuality/companion stage, which is followed by parenthood.

Do you recognize in yourself a preferred stage of development? Do you recognize in a love partner a preferred stage?

These developmental love patterns follow a maturation process, a steady development of attachments over time accompanied by certain behaviors that, for most of us, are relatively similar. Although every human being has a unique, personal development, we can profit by knowing about human patterns.

If we skip or only partly satisfy one of these developmental stages—symbiotic love, affectionate/responsive, seductive/possessive, chum/chum, lover/lover, mutuality/companion—we may expend great energy at a later time in our lives trying to go back to complete a stage of development or kind of love left undone. We can get stuck in an uncompleted development stage, fixated on the fulfillment of one kind of love that interferes with future relationships. The Don Juan and the seductive female seem stuck in an unfinished stage.

## Mature Love

Mature love takes time. Like planting a seed in the proper soil followed by constant care and nourishment, love can grow. It requires many shared experiences and, after many sacrifices, builds up gradually over time. Mutual interests, genuinely complementary personalities, and the ability to enjoy the companionship of another person all nurture love. Love must be earned; it cannot be bought or forced. Love is a passionate interest in another person.

Unrequited love is the tragic experience of loving and being unloved in return. The degree of pain depends on the person's attitude and self-esteem. Near a state of emotional collapse, a young woman jilted by her sweetheart a week before the wedding returned all the wedding presents and wrote each invited guest that the wedding was canceled.

Canceled weddings are not rare. Often, self-confidence is shaken and self-esteem damaged. The loss of loved ones through death, the end of a relationship, and even divorce are universal, timeless experiences. But most people learn to love again.

Human beings have a great potential to heal and grow. At a time of crisis, when a loved one leaves, some persons feel they will never recover. Sometimes a lack of trust, disillusionment, and a sense of failure follow the end of a love affair. Yet often a past love experience adds to a future love, making it better, more secure, and more intelligent than would have been otherwise possible.

We can never wholly know ourselves or any other person. In our longing to experience complete intimacy with the self and with a soul mate who also knows and loves us unconditionally, we often search in the wrong places. Those of us who strive to find a soul mate who truly understands our inner core are doomed to disappointment. The old adage "Time heals all wounds" does not prepare us for the emotional scars that often lie below the surface of our consciousness.

Everyone experiences moments of loneliness. Philosopher Peter Koestenbaum says loneliness tells us no one else in the whole world is like us. A human being is a separate entity. Those who seek to alleviate loneliness through love, often experience this search as a crisis in intimacy.

Most of us can recall a time in childhood when someone held us in their arms and said, "Don't worry, darling, I will take care of you." The child in us, hidden inside an adult body, longs for that safety and caring. As adults, this longing is mixed with many other motives. Essentially, however, the permanence and security of a mature love provide the safety and caring most of us seek. The search for intimacy is a search for both a soul mate and meaning in life. Many of us try to satisfy both searches through loving relationships.

In our interactions with others, we share ideas and try to change attitudes and influence behavior. At the same time, we continue to want the approval, love, and affection of those early years. When we are truly understood, we feel safe from hostile forces. If we find someone who affirms us and our reality, we want that person to be available to us whenever we need support.

We expect this person to stimulate our minds and bodies. We not only want an affectionate, intelligent person but also an attractive person. The good feeling we experience as physical attraction requires that our loved one be an erotic sex partner. Often, we feel, our own worth is reflected by the attractiveness of our loved one.

We further expect this person to carry out certain kinds of behaviors, such as giving flowers and gifts, defined by the culture as evidence of love. Someone who waits on us or who provides services like cleaning and cooking or fixing our car demonstrates love. We also expect this person to be faithful and loyal to us and available whenever we need him or her. We want to be able to count on our loved one.

Moreover, since some experts tell us the best relationships are ones with total candor and honesty, ones in which nothing is hidden and everything is put out on the table, we expect perfect communication in our relationships.

With our loved one, we expect to be truly ourselves, to be spontaneous, without any game playing, role playing, phoniness, or hypocrisy. In sum, we expect someone who loves us to provide us with social, economic, physical, and emotional security, services and gifts, sexual satisfaction, and intellectual excitement and stimulation, all in addition to fun and companionship.

We go into relationships expecting the all-loving, unconditional love we received from our mothers, the friendship we had with our peers, and the romance and passion we knew during our adolescent years. We want all these things, and the experts tell us everything is possible if we work hard enough at it.

Then, we ask, "Why can't we find intimacy? Why is love so often full of anguish, disappointment, and disillusionment?"

Love cannot bear the burdens of our wants, hopes, and expectations. Some experts suggest we can learn skills for relating and loving and intimacy, as we learn to ride a bike or drive a car. For temporary improvements, developing these skills might help. But we will not be good candidates for fulfilling, satisfying, mature love until we stop expecting others to meet our many demands for mothering, security, friendship, and mating.

Although we value the ideals of perfect love, mature love is more realistic, gives more and demands less, forgives and accepts imperfections in both the self and the loved one.

According to the 1985 census, 85 to 90 percent of all Americans get married at least once in their lives. Considering that many of the 10 to 15 percent who do not marry are mentally or physically handicapped, and others "marry" the church, we can conclude almost all Americans get married. Since most of us will marry, are married, or have been married, we look, in the next chapter, at marriage in the United States as it was, as it is, and as it might be.

# Intimacy and Marriage 6

*To have and to hold from this day forward,*
*for better, for worse, for richer, for poorer,*
*in sickness, and in health,*
*to love and to cherish . . .*
Book of Common Prayer

Americans are convinced love and marriage, like "a horse and carriage," go together. Matrimony, we believe, offers the happiness and security we long for. Traditional, economic reasons for marriage—a strong, healthy mate; children who contribute to building an estate; financial security; and support in one's old-age—have been replaced by personal reasons.

Of all the reasons given for marriage today, love is the most often stated. Yet Dr. John Hudson, past president of the American Association of Marriage and Family Counselors, says in approximately 25 percent of all marriages described as "happy," one or both persons said they were not in love. Still, love continues to be the foundation for a belief in marriage. Most Americans believe a stable marriage is the best way to live.

As an institution, marriage is constantly changing. In the 1950s, 96 percent of all people of childbearing age were married and believed it would last forever. Getting married represented the transition to adulthood and, therefore, was expected. Eager to leave home and become adults, many young people got married. The goals of marriage were security, stability, loyalty, togetherness, and permanence. Husbands were breadwinners; wives, housekeepers and mothers. Through mass media, young women learned marriage not only brought adulthood but also a beautiful home, wonderful children, and "happiness-ever-after."

In the 1960s, the postwar baby boomers came of age. They rebelled against past values. War in Vietnam and affluence brought freedom marches and restlessness. The Growth Movement, with its multiple kinds of experiments brought group marriages, communes, and open marriages, which allowed each partner to be free "to do his or her own thing."

In the l970s, the Human Potential Movement, with its emphasis on experimentation, freedom, and multiple options, flourished. One popular slogan of "The Me Generation" became, "You do your thing, and I'll do mine." Over time, most couples found these new experiments didn't work.

Today, in the 1980s, divorce—not togetherness—has become a national concern. According to recent statistics, 50 percent of first marriages end in divorce. However, Americans believe in marriage so much that 75 percent of all people who get divorced remarry within five years. It is statistically likely that by l990 more people will be in a second marriage than in a first one. Second marriages include step-children and blended families with their own special challenges.

More than ever before, marriage today means making choices, such as whether to marry later in life, more than once, or not at all. Many young people are living longer with their parents. Statistically, women under the age of 20 have four times as great a chance of divorce as those who marry between the ages of 22 and 24. Young women are opting for education or careers before marriage. As a result, the average marrying age is rising.

When marriages end, divorced men and women sometimes move back home to live with their parents. And more people are choosing not to marry at all. Despite these changes, we still believe in marriage and hope for the best—to be part of a married couple who share love and loyalty, if not for a lifetime, than for as long as the marriage lasts.

## Love Then Marriage

Today, a shared, equalitarian relationship in a marriage is the stated goal of most Americans. Most young people believe all they have to do is find the "right" man or woman to fall in love with; then marriage will automatically bring happiness. We believe marriage is the answer to getting what we want.

According to a recent survey, 90 percent of teenagers want to get married someday. And 92 percent think they will get what they want out of life. These statistics come from young people who have watched their own or their friends' parents go through divorces and live with disappointments in work and careers.

Marriage and family have been and will doubtlessly continue to be high on the American list of values. When a large sample of brilliant, successful, middle-aged men and women were asked to look back on what was most satisfying in their lives, the vast majority said their families had been the most fulfilling and satisfying—more so than their professional accomplishments, community status, and financial success.

Perhaps for some of us, the American Dream of success and happiness through marriage can be a self-fulfilling prophecy. We Americans tend to be relatively optimistic about our personal lives even when the external world remains uncontrollable. We believe in marriage; most Americans who get divorced marry again.

On the other hand, being single is more accepted today than in the past. Asked why they were *not* married, a group of single people—some never married and some previously married—gave these reasons:

- I don't want the hassles, boredom, or responsibilities.
- I don't want to answer to someone else, to have to consider them all the time.
- I want to put my time and energy into my education or career.
- I love my freedom, independence, autonomy.
- I like the flexibility, the mobility of being single.
- I like having my options open and having more choices.
- I like to date a variety of people.
- I don't want to put all my money into a kitty.
- I don't like giving up control; I'm not ready for personal ties.
- I'm afraid of losing my own identity.

In the past, single people who didn't marry were thought to be unwanted losers. Today, we accept that many unmarried people are single by choice. We now recognize more lifestyles to choose from. Americans are staying single longer and getting married later than ever before. Still, most of us will marry at least once.

## Asking the Right Questions

Many people believe they aren't married because they "just haven't found the right person yet." Most people fail to acknowledge that perhaps *they* are not the "right" people to be married—at least not at this time in their lives.

---

Instead of asking, "Why marry?" ask yourself, "Am I the kind of person who should get married?"

- Do I get depressed if I have to spend a holiday alone?
- Do I feel uncomfortable going to a theater alone?
- Do I need another person to want to work toward my goals?
- Do I need another person to help me make decisions?
- Do I dislike sleeping alone and eating alone?
- Am I willing to share my money with another person?
- Do I want children?
- Am I willing to make compromises?
- Do I prefer a stable relationship with one person?

Even if all of your answers suggest you are the type of person to marry, if you choose a mate who does not want to be married, your marriage will probably not work.

---

According to sociologists Burgess and Wallin, happily married persons have the following characteristics:

- Emotional dependence
- Emotional stability
- Willingness to yield
- Consideration for others
- Companionableness
- Self-confidence

A study of shy persons with low self-esteem found that shyness appears to prevent a person from entering long-term relationships such as marriage or friendship. A shy person may not be likely to initiate or intensify contacts with others because of extreme self-consciousness or fear of rejection. It's important to ask, "Am I the kind of person who should be married?"

Another important question is "What kind of person should I marry?" The answer depends on knowing who you are, what you want, and what you value most. Important mating factors include appearance, personality, money, sex, affection, social status, and how much each person values marriage. Research indicates the partner who wants marriage the most or who is most excited about getting married considers himself or herself the happier of the two during the marriage.

The kind of companionate love that works best in a marriage

requires suitable mates. If you prize appearance, you are unlikely to feel good married to someone you do not think is attractive regardless of how much money or social status he or she has. However, no matter how attractive another person is, if you feel he or she has a repellent personality, you probably will not think of the person as a suitable marital partner for you.

On the West Coast, there is a thriving business in mail-order brides. American men are "ordering" *subservient*, shy Asian women who want money, status, and U.S. citizenship. Most of the men are over 40, and most of the Asian brides are under 25. Both parties believe they are choosing the kind of marriage partner they want. But after these Asian women get to the United States and meet American women, some of the Asian women change. One husband, when asked how satisfied he was with his mail-order bride, answered, "She's not as subservient as I wanted."

One problem with personal growth is that values change. What a 20-year-old person wants in a marriage is usually not what a 40-year-old wants. To ask "What kind of person do I want to marry?" is a double-edged sword. If your description or image is rigid or unrealistic, no person is likely to fit it. Or if you find the person you are looking for, he or she may not be interested in you.

Researchers tell us those who score high in personality, appearance, money, sex, affection, and social status expect to marry someone of equal value. Although all humans are valuable as persons, in marriage, we look for mates having equivalent market value.

In most marriages, one partner loves more than the other. Often, one person is more satisfied with marriage. The one more satisfied is also the more vulnerable, for he or she has the most to lose if the relationship ends. Intellectual, physical, emotional, and financial investments in a marriage are rarely equal.

To live with another person peacefully requires some degree of compatibility of needs, values, interests, and personalities. If we fall in love with an incompatible person, we will probably find it difficult to live together 365 days a year for even a few years let alone for a lifetime.

Professor Robert Winch of Northwestern University says, "The love of man for woman and woman for man is basically self-serving. Its primary purpose is to benefit the lover, not the beloved." Through his research study of 50 married couples, he found that persons who like to dominate, teach, or direct—whether male or female—usually choose persons who like to be steered, instructed, or criticized.

In the most successful marriages, one spouse has a strong need for recognition, whereas the other usually has a scant need; an easygoing attitude mates with a flashing temper. In effect, people who marry persons with complementary personalities are more likely to have their needs met.

The need theory does little to help people whose needs change over time. The paradox of need-fulfillment is that once a need for something or someone is satisfied, the need no longer exists. When a need dissipates, we go on to fulfill unmet needs.

Another important question to ask is "When should I get married?" Timing is critical. A person too immature to marry at 20, may be an excellent candidate for marriage after ten years of single living. If a person has just ended a love relationship or marriage, he or she is unlikely to be a good candidate for a serious, new relationship. There is a period after the end of a deep involvement called "the fertile void" during which a person renews the self as an individual before being ready for a commitment to a new relationship.

Some questions to ask yourself about the right time to get married are

- Am I ready to take on the responsibilities of marriage?
- Do I want to be considerate of another person's feelings?
- Do I want to help another person reach his or her goals?
- Am I willing to settle down, to maintain some degree of stability?
- Am I ready to make a permanent commitment to one person?
- Do I want to be responsible for and to another person?
- Is this the right time in my life to get married?
- Am I financially stable enough to finance a marriage?

Psychologists and sociologists have studied mate-selection patterns of needs and expectations. Assuming you are the kind of person who wants to be married and have chosen a mate who wants to be married, and assuming this is the right time for both of you, marital satisfaction often depends on each of you playing the role expected of you.

Marriage role expectations are seldom discussed. Each partner must ask questions to get a clear picture of what the other wants from marriage. If a woman envisions herself as a successful entrepreneur while her husband expects her to spend her days making his home a castle in which to entertain his friends and business associates, their visions of the marriage they want are incompatible. If a man wants children, but his wife does not want to be tied down with the responsibilities of raising a family, their different visions of marriage will leave one or the other unfulfilled. This lack of fulfillment may eventually destroy the marriage.

---

Discuss the following questions:

• What kind of marriage do I want?
• What kind of marriage does my partner want?
• What roles do I want to play in a marriage?
• What roles does my partner expect me to take?

Compromises can eventually result in one or the other partner feeling resentful. Regularly adjusting marital roles and expectations and renewing talks about needs and wants can help.

---

Mate-selection patterns of needs and expectations differ from marriage roles. Satisfaction in a marriage depends not only on choosing a mate that meets individual needs and expectations but also on each partner's playing those roles expected by the other.

Because people change over time, marriage role expectations differ according to the stage of a marriage. A married couple often has the most difficulty during transitions from one stage of a marriage to another. The first year of a marriage has its own peculiar set of problems, which are different from those of the 5th to 10th years, 20th to 30th years, and 40th to 50th years of marriage.

---

Assume the following of you and your mate:

• You both believe in marriage.
• You each believe you are the right kind of person to be married.

• You both have the same vision of the kind of marriage you want and the roles you expect to play.

Now ask each other, "Why do you want to be married?" Is it so that you will have someone

• To love and who will love you
• To share your life with
• To have children with and who will help you raise them
• You can take care of and who will take care of you
• Who will be a companion and friend
• Who will eat, sleep, go places, and do things with you so that you won't be lonely
• Who will satisfy your physical and sexual needs

To minimize misunderstandings, it is important to ask your mate his or her reasons for marrying, keeping in mind that most of us are vulnerable to self-deception.

---

Three common "wrong" reasons for marrying are to acquire a regular sex partner, obtain economic or emotional security, and escape from loneliness. These can seem like sound or satisfactory reasons, but someone who marries to escape from some sort of unpleasantness rarely experiences an enduring or satisfying marriage.

Reasons for marrying are multiple and complex. Researchers have found that men and women get married for different reasons. Women usually say they want to get married to have a home and family. Men more often mention sex, service, and companionship.

Romantic love often leads to making love. In a culture that has not entirely sanctioned sex without marriage, many young people dream about falling in love and getting married. Having sex without love and marriage is, for many Americans, unacceptable; however, sex seldom holds a marriage together.

### Two Marriages—His and Hers

In the past, men considered marriage a trap, and women considered it salvation. A single man was an "eligible bachelor," whereas a single woman was an "old maid" not attractive enough to catch a man. Women tended to think they were nothing, worthless, without value unless they had a man.

The paradox is that, according to sociologist Jessie Bernard in *The Future of Marriage,* marriage is physically, socially, and psychologically good for men while, statistically, marriage literally makes thousands of women sick. Married women have poorer mental and emotional health than single women. Three times as many married as single women show severe neurotic symptoms, anxiety, depression, phobias, and emotional distress.

Tsipora Peskin, professor at the University of California's Institute of Human Development in Berkeley, has collected data from a 40-year study of marriages. She says marriage is two worlds, his and hers. Men and women reach these worlds by different paths. Traditionally, marriage has been the most important part of a woman's life. Even if she works outside the home, a wife performs household duties, takes care of her husband and children, and provides a well-ordered home. Wives who remain married, according to Peskin's study, rate low in self-assertion, self-indulgence, and independence. They are more submissive and conventional than women who do not stay married.

In contrast, men often see marriage as merely a companion to their careers and other interests. Statistically, married men live longer, healthier, happier lives than single men. Peskin found that the men who were rated as dependent, indecisive, and uncomfortable with complexity were likely to stay married. Economic success, job satisfaction, and their wives' forbearance may contribute to married men's happiness.

Despite these research findings, married men and women say they are happily married.

---

Among researchers' findings are that

- Few men or women are capable of giving unconditional love indefinitely without any expectations.
- The more we are willing to give, the more we can expect in return, but the giving and getting will rarely be equal.
- Although we cannot have everything, often we can get in marriage those things most important to us.
- Persons who demand from themselves or others love without thought of return are deceiving themselves.
- Biologically, we seek pleasure and avoid pain; therefore, we

must make compromises in marriage and acknowledge we give pleasure to get pleasure.
- An unequal relationship causes pain. The one who gives the most feels resentful, and the one who gets the most feels guilty.
- To eliminate inequities in a marriage, people tend to even the score, convince themselves it is fair, or end the relationship.

---

Sociologist Peter Blau, from Columbia University, says we end up with mates we deserve. According to the principles of the marketplace, the most desirable suitors get the most desirable mates. Those who are less attractive, intelligent, or understanding end up with lovers who are less attractive, intelligent, or understanding.

To find out if these tradeoffs produced happy marriages, a team of researchers asked 600 men and women about their relationships. They were asked to compare how much they gave to the relationship with how much they got from it.

Each person rated his or her contributions on a scale from "My partner gets a much better . . . somewhat better . . . slightly better deal" to "I am getting a slightly better . . . somewhat better . . . much better deal." Then they were asked how they felt about how much they put into the relationships and how much they got out. Feelings were listed as "contented . . . happy . . . angry . . . guilty."

The researchers found that people in *equitable relationships* felt content or happy. Those who thought they were getting more than they deserved felt guilt. And those who thought they were getting less than they deserved felt resentment.

Nearly four months later, the researchers contacted the respondents again and asked them how much sex they had in their relationships. In general, those couples who reported equitable relationships had more sex than those who reported inequitable ones. Couples in inequitable relationships were less likely to say they both wanted sex.

One psychologist says when people interact with one another, they tend to give what they get, both in amount and in kind. Although we may deny it, all of us seem to have our own bookkeeping system for love and pain. Over time, if the books don't balance, we do something to create equity, or we leave.

Reports of changes in equitable relationships indicate balances get upset. For example, the man who loses his job and the fat woman who loses weight no longer contribute to their relationships as they did before. Couples either find some way of restoring equity, such as giving up power or getting something more out of the relationship, or they end the relationship.

Research studies in the United States, Canada, Germany, and Japan show that men and women date and marry people who are about as physically attractive as they are. Other assets such as physical health, money, status, intelligence, popularity, and education are used to create equity. Sometimes one person gives more love so that the partner will tolerate flaws. Although the amount and kind of giving and getting cannot be dealt with logically, they affect both the endurance and quality of marriages.

Perhaps the most hazardous element in a marriage is change. What we want, what we expect, and who we are all change. Seldom do two people in a marriage change at the same time, in the same direction, or to the same degree. Thus flexibility and adaptation to change by at least one partner may be crucial to the survival of the marriage.

### When the Magic Fades

One young man writes,

> I have been married two years to a beautiful woman. For the first year, our relationship was pure magic. But this past year, I find myself increasingly disenchanted. I feel a powerful craving to find other women in an attempt to bring back the magic that makes me feel alive and whole. Now that it is missing from my life, I hunger for its completeness. I wish I could fall back into love with my wife. What can I do?

Marriage is an attempt to create a growing relationship and cannot give us the "magic" of total fulfillment. Those parts of us that seek completion in marriage do so because we lack an internal balance of opposites within ourselves.

Perhaps our most unrealistic demand is to continue feeling passionate love for our partners. In a study of 453 engaged or recently married persons, a scant 18 percent felt their emotional needs were being well satisfied by their mates.

No one person can satisfy all of our emotional needs. We were brought up on fairy-tale love stories, and we desperately want to believe a good marriage will be happy forever. Strong beliefs and hopes grow into expectations. Therefore, we expect a good marriage to be passionate, exclusive, and permanent.

Experience does not necessarily persuade us to abandon our fantasies for reality. Some women compensate by reading romance novels, and some men through pornography. These and other compensations can contribute to permanence in marriage. Some measure of sacrifice, endurance, self-discipline, and compromise, as well as the willingness to live with imperfections in self, other, and the relationship itself contribute to longevity in marriage.

### Companionate Marriage

In *Marriage & Work in America,* Joseph Veroff and Sheila Feld found that, in marriage, men prefer sexuality to companionship, whereas women prefer companionship to sexuality. Wives said companionship was more important than love, understanding, or standard of living.

Although companionate marriage is best achieved when partners are alike, sexuality flourishes when partners are different. Excitement, thrills, and romance live in most people's fantasies. The best marriages combine sex and companionship in proportions pleasing to both partners.

In a nationwide survey published in the February 1984 issue of *Ladies Home Journal,* based on responses of 86,000 readers, women were asked what they would be most likely to do if they had a few free hours alone with their husbands. Thirty-three percent of the women under 35 answered, "make love." Only 25 percent of those 35 to 45 gave this answer, and a mere 10 percent of those over 45, most of whom answered "watch TV."

Everybody gets some things they want from a partner and gives up other things. The willingness to compromise is directly related to the length of relationships. Ideally, beginnings are beautiful, even magical. Then the magic often transforms itself into a deeper, more enduring, stronger kind of love.

Marriage is many things other than love; it is a whole pattern of attachments. Marriage itself does not create difficulties—people do. We create our own difficulties within the structure of marriage. Our problems are personal and include distrust, perfectionism, criticism, blame, and unrealistic expectations.

How-to articles in magazines and books about making marriage last tell us we must work to keep our relationships robust. They tell us we must accept each other's flaws, adapt to each other's disagreeable habits, and appreciate each other's good qualities. They tell us working at a relationship means constant attention to little "tricks" to keep passion alive. In the end, however, daily living requires that we replace passion with compatibility and companionship for the reward of permanence.

A marriage can be experienced as a working partnership, a joint effort to help each other face difficulties and achieve satisfactions. It's agreeing to face obstacles together, to be on the same side. If either partner in a marriage finally learns he or she *can* live without the support of another, that person is free to be in a marriage by choice, which creates the best of both possible worlds. To transcend both dependence and independence is possible though difficult.

In lasting, satisfactory marriages, friendship replaces passion. The lover turns into a friend. The intensity of love is supplanted by peaceful attachment. Many couples find that a friend is what they wanted all along. We value shared understandings, emotions, and habits. We want someone to share our interests, keep us from feeling lonely, and help us achieve the things we want. Once we acknowledge we are not going to get everything we want, we settle for those things most important to us.

Often, married men and women get all the challenge they can handle through their work. At home, they want peace and tranquillity. A husband and wife often enjoy routine and simply being able to count on each other. They prefer a serene, unruffled flow. They can share day-to-day pleasures without incessant conversation. In fact, in the simple silence of a loyal companion, they find peace.

In later years, married couples expect to spend the rest of their lives together reminiscing, looking back with pride on the years spent together. Our culture rewards and celebrates long marriages regardless of their quality. Making a marriage last is assumed to be a measure of success rather than endurance. A long marriage is considered one kind of accomplishment.

At the turn of this century, when the life span was 49 years, a couple who married at the age of 20 could live together for 30 years. Today, the average life span for a woman is 77 years and for a man, 69 years. Thus a couple who married at 20 could spend more than 50 years together. Recently, two couples were documented as having been married 80 and 82 years.

We live in a culture that teaches us to be successful and exhorts us that marriage must last a lifetime, so many people do all they can to keep their marriages going. Studies of marital happiness have found that the longer a couple is wed, the less satisfaction or dissatisfaction each partner claims to feel. Yet some couples report the later years of married life are the happiest.

To find out what differentiates satisfied from dissatisfied older couples, Purdue University psychologist Clifford Swenson conducted a series of studies involving nearly 1,000 couples. He found that, over the course of a lifetime together, both the amount of love expressed between husband and wife *and* the number of problems they have decline. Less appears to be happening between them either positive or negative. Most older people find more peace and tranquillity than they experienced at any other time in life.

In another study, Robert O. Blood and Donald M. Wolfe studied 900 marriages. They interviewed a random sample of Detroit women to find out how satisfied they were with their marriages. They found that marital satisfaction sags steadily with the passing decades. After 20 years of marriage, only 6 percent said they were "very satisfied," and 21 percent were conspicuously dissatisfied. Blood and Wolfe suggested *disengagement* occurs—a progressive withdrawal of the couple from mutual interaction. Still, about 70 percent of the women said they were satisfied or neutral.

As time passes, partners spend less and less time together, and when they are together, they pay less and less attention to each other. One explanation could be that couples married more than 20 years feel secure enough in their marriage to be content without the immoderate talk and constant togetherness of earlier years. Perhaps they have finally come to terms with the freedom to follow their own interests.

Many husbands and wives find gratification outside the marriage relationship: interests, friends, work, adult children. About the time a woman's children leave home, she wants to travel and explore the outside world, while her husband, who has worked all of his life, longs to become a homebody. Their hopes for the future are not always the same. Some couples find ways to fulfill their individual needs, whereas others compromise to make their marriages work.

## Marriages End

All marriages end—either by death or divorce. In the past, those that ended in death were labeled successful, and those that ended in divorce were labeled failures. Although some married couples will stay together until death, with our present extended life span, expecting many marriages to last until one of the partners dies is unrealistic.

Most primitive societies have had higher rates of marital dissolution than we have today. And several nations have exceeded our present divorce rate at some time in their history. Divorce is not a new phenomenon.

Today, we talk about divorce as *an institution*. According to our census, one out of every two marriages ends in divorce. We can also safely say some marriages that do *not* end are often held together despite disillusionment and dissatisfaction. Among the many reasons people stay together, security, permanence, stability, and religion play a large part.

For many people, security and permanence are a fair exchange for unfulfilled needs. They would rather live out their lives in a less than satisfying marriage than risk the unknown. They often intuitively know the grass is not greener on the other side of the fence.

People's standards for marriage are higher today than at any other time in history. We often compare ourselves to our parent's generation. We believe in commitment but are unwilling to tolerate what our parents tolerated. In the past, men and women alike lived with alcoholism, physical beatings, and mates who played around. Today, when things become intolerable, we are more apt to leave.

Researchers have recently found a direct connection between the divorce rate and the economy. In times of depression, there are fewer divorces. Divorces are expensive. When people cannot afford to divorce, they stay together. During times of affluence, however, the divorce rate soars.

Attachments to material possessions keep some marriages together. Getting married means, in part, two people working together to buy a house, furniture, cars, and other possessions. Another common reason people give for staying married is "the children." Men and women who do not want to divide up their assets or be separated from their children often avoid divorce and endure the marriage.

Religious beliefs hold other marriages together. Ending a marriage is absolutely forbidden by some churches. To disobey one's religion proves more difficult for some persons than staying in an unhappy marriage.

One of the four main reasons men cite for divorce is infidelity. Extramarital sex is often said to destroy a marriage, but many claim it is dishonesty that creates walls between people in a relationship.

Alfred Kinsey and his colleagues concluded that adultery can be fairly harmless in a marriage if the spouse doesn't find out. In collecting data for his study on males, Kinsey didn't ask men about infidelity. But when he studied females, he realized these questions were important to ask.

About half the women who had affairs reported that their husbands did not know about them. Nearly 9 percent of the women worried that their husbands might know, and 40 percent were certain they knew. When they did know, 58 percent of the couples had only "minor" difficulty, and 42 percent "serious" difficulty.

Kinsey concluded that 71 percent of the time, extramarital relationships caused no marital problems—either the partner did not find out or did not care. Yet in the Kinsey research, there is conflicting information.

When asked, "Did *your* extramarital intercourse figure in your divorce?" women answered it was relatively unimportant. When asked, "Did your *spouse's* extramarital intercourse have any effect on your divorce?" they said it was important. When *they* had the extramarital sex, they said it had little effect on the divorce. But when they knew their spouse had the extramarital sex, it was a very important factor.

Monogamy provides emotional security and stability in a marriage at the cost of giving up certain personal needs and satisfactions. Serial monogamy—marrying more than once—provides romance, variety, and challenge at the cost of the guilt, trauma, and pain of divorce. Adultery, which attempts to satisfy emotional needs through sex outside the marriage, also exacts its price.

So many myths surround the topic of extramarital affairs that almost everyone has a different answer rooted in some cliché. The person who says, "Everyone plays around" rationalizes and justifies his or her behavior. False generalizations like, "Men can't be trusted" add suspicion and distrust to any relationship.

Though infidelity in a marriage is not inevitable, thinking about it is. To be attracted to people other than a spouse is hardly uncommon. Even the most monogamous person occasionally finds others of the opposite sex attractive and may even fantasize a beautiful romance without acting it out. On the other hand, extramarital affairs are so common that we search to understand the complex motivations behind them.

Some people experience loving two people at the same time. Although many unfaithful spouses are firmly committed to their marriages, the excitement of being found attractive contributes to the fascination and intoxication of being newly in love. Abraham Maslow says, "It blinds people to their lovers' faults and reminds them of the days when they were young and carefree." Yet even the glow of an extramarital affair fades with time. If a marriage has value, no one can compete with a marriage partner who tolerates a spouse's affair.

An alarming number of husbands and wives blame themselves for their spouses' infidelities, yet unfaithful spouses are often reluctant to seek a divorce. Self-reproaching spouses play games with themselves, as does the unfaithful spouse who finds fault in a mate as an excuse for an extramarital affair. Rarely is sex the real motivation behind an extramarital affair.

Many marriages can survive an extramarital affair if the marriage is worth saving. Sometimes, an affair results in the husband and wife beginning to talk and listen to each other on a deeper level than at any other time in the marriage. Other times, the affair is an excuse to end a marriage.

Reasons given for ending a marriage are often filled with oversimplifications and rationalizations. Discrepancies between what people do and what they say support the theory that self-deception contributes to divorce.

Divorced people fall into two categories: those who leave and those who are left. Some people pretend it is a mutual decision. But if one person does not want to be married, there is no marriage. Those who leave suffer guilt, whereas those who are left eventually feel intense anger and resentment though often submerged under defenses.

One middle-aged man who was left said,

> I felt absolute panic. I started out feeling as if I had cancer. I seriously considered suicide. I went through many stages. After some time, I ended up feeling as if the cancer was really only a case of acne.

This man's ex-wife said,

> After the children left, I felt trapped, restricted, unable to be who I wanted to be. Now I feel wonderful—free, growing, changing—like a bird who has just learned to fly.

Divorce as an institution reminds us marriages may not last any longer than anything else does in this world. Past roles can be discarded. Unsatisfying personality patterns can be exchanged for new identities. One woman said,

> It feels like a movement is going on, like a dance in which everyone is taking a step to the left. Being divorced is like joining a club. It seems to be happening to everyone.

A mutual agreement often begins as a harmony of feelings in the present with hopes for the future. We each make many commitments in life—to the self, to a job, to others in relationships, to a marriage and family. For many reasons, when conditions change, commitments change. When a commitment to self conflicts with a commitment to another, keeping either commitment can be destructive to the other.

In our culture, we accept many kinds of broken agreements, such as students who drop courses and employees who quit jobs. Yet many people still believe a marriage commitment must not be violated, as if the belief alone will make the marriage last forever irrespective of cost.

A contract is a legal document, a binding agreement between two persons. The law provides methods to end contracts. We accept the breaking of business contracts but continue to have rigid attitudes toward marriage contracts. Thus we suffer a great deal of pain when they are broken or changed.

Today, aware as we are that no one can promise to feel something forever, the phrase most often deleted from modern wedding ceremonies is the promise to stay together "till death us do part."

Every commitment restricts freedom. Caring for another person requires some submission of individuality for mutual gain. A relationship takes time, space, energy. It cannot provide personal meaning or prevent feelings of loneliness. It must be shared by mutual consent. When the commitment is no longer mutual, divorce or disengagement follows.

Commitments kept out of duty or obligation usually result in rebellion, frustration, guilt, resentment, depression, and emotional separation. Physicians find that some persons who remain in a bad marriage become physically ill. A destructive marriage can harm your health and even shorten your life. Ending a marriage can be an act of emotional and physical survival.

Like a dependency addiction, the end of a marriage often brings withdrawal symptoms and intense physical and emotional pain. The bewilderment we feel when marriage is not what we hoped and dreamed is often followed by depression. Doubt and disappointment accompanied by guilt make us ask, "What's wrong with me?" "Am I unlovable?" Or worse, "Am I unable to love?"

Several research studies confirm that unmarried women experience less depression than married women; however, unmarried men experience more depression than married men. Apparently marriage frees men from stress while placing emotionally stressful demands on women. Although females avoid depressed males, ironically, males do not avoid depressed females. Studies show single men are less happy than married men, but single women are as happy or happier than married women. The unhappiest women, studies show, are nonworking and married.

Lack of confidence, lowered self-esteem, insecurity, and confusion follow the dissolution of a marriage. Recently divorced people often join groups to give one another support. The divorced person learns these feelings are normal and precede a readiness for growth and change.

The divorce rate in second marriages is higher than that in first marriages. Perhaps this is because although we believe in marriage, most of us not only survive a divorce we also learn how strong we are and that we can handle diversity. Meeting and solving problems in life gives us a chance to learn and grow in our own independence.

Although 70 percent of divorces in the United States occur before the partners reach middle age, as working women become financially independent, middle-aged divorce is becoming increasingly common. In the past, middle-aged men were more likely to end their marriages, but today, self-supporting middle-aged women are more likely to leave.

A new study finds that women who divorce in middle age adjust better than men. Penn State sociologists Gunhild Hagestad and Michael Smyer interviewed 93 men and women between the ages of 41 and 61 who had been married an average of 25 years. They found that most of the women knew ten years before their divorces that their marriages were not working, whereas most of the men knew less than three years before. Thus the women prepared more. They began to adjust both emotionally and financially, which made their transitions from married to single life easier. Starting over, the researchers concluded, seems to be a lot easier for females.

Some people respond to change and stress better than others. These people have an inner sense of security, an inner source of energy. They have some internal response structure or sense of roots that gives them stability and continuity within themselves.

Surveys depend on the population that answers them. In a *Redbook* survey of more than 50,000 Americans on happiness, the happiest group were married men, and the second happiest were single women over 50. Married women ranked themselves lower in happiness. Yet in the February 1983 issue of *Ladies Home Journal*, of the 83,000 younger, married women who replied, 82 percent considered their marriages happy, even when they reported sexual difficulties or dysfunctions.

Discrepancies in voluntary, self-report studies like these may be due to biases, different populations, or the wording of questions, yet these surveys indicate certain social and personal trends.

A marriage can be a success whether it lasts 5 or 50 years. To stay in a marriage that leaves one person unfulfilled for the sake of the partner is martyrdom and emotional suicide. In these cases, divorce can be the first step toward a more fulfilling lifestyle.

Most young people want to be and will be married. Though half those marriages may end in divorce, that does not mean they are unsuccessful or wrong in their time. We must guard against people who use such expressions as *fail, marital despair,* and *where things go wrong and how to make them right.* These persons demonstrate their own biased belief systems.

Even without love, marriages can be successful when both partners care about and respect each other, fulfill each other's needs, and provide each other with experiences to learn and grow from. People can stay together if they are understanding, caring, respectful, and willing to work out the problems of living together.

Whether married or single, people change. Ideally, two persons will both change and enjoy each other's changes, but changes and needs are seldom synchronized. The strength of long-term marriages is not necessarily that those couples have no bad times but that nobody leaves.

A marriage is an entirely individual construction built by two unique people. No universal answers exist about why people marry, why some stay together, or why some divorce, just as no universal prescription for happiness exists.

Despite increasing risks, Americans will continue to marry. People yearn for intimacy and companionship. We want a stable household or home, a base to confidently explore the world from, knowing someone is waiting for us. In an unstable, uncertain world, the need for an anchor becomes especially important. Marriage also provides an accounting for kinship ties, keeps track of blood relationships, and guarantees ancestry.

In the future, divorce will not necessarily increase or become a universal experience. Divorce does not mean we are not loving persons. It may simply be, for some, a part of the marital experience. Most people will spend much of their adult lives married—some in one marriage and others in two or more.

Two individuals—a man and a woman—take hands and agree to go for a walk. One walks more slowly and the other more rapidly than they would walk by themselves. Each accommodates the other. Later they may decide to explore the path at their own pace. "I'll wait for you at the top of the hill," the faster walker may say.

When one of them wishes to go right and the other wishes to go left, it does not mean the partnership is a failure if they do not continue on the same path together forever. We cannot predict our future—neither as individuals nor as couples. Love and marriage are only one part of life. Our lives and our relationships must be designed and redesigned. Since divorce is a freer choice today, lasting marriages are freely chosen. To be married today means choosing marriage for however long it lasts for whatever it has to offer. When we marry, we choose marriage and the person we marry as the best of all our alternatives at that particular time in our lives.

In the future, as a result of people living longer and changing mates to suit the seasons of their lives, serial marriage may become a normal, planned part of adulthood. Children will grow up with several sets of parents and an assortment of half- and step-siblings. Through counseling and genuinely shared custody of children, divorcing couples will be able to put an end to their anger and pain more quickly. Positive developments through patterns of divorce and remarriage may result in a whole new kinship network.

Persons with a strong sense of self, a developed self-esteem, can enjoy the transformations that occur in relationships and come out stronger, more experienced, and wiser than before. They will discover it is more important *to be the right person* than it is to find the right person.

In its complexity, intimacy takes many forms: emotional, intellectual, and physical. For most of us, marriage and sexuality are intimately connected. Some experts say we spend more time studying, researching, and discussing the human sexual act than performing it.

Because physical intimacy often troubles us, in the next chapter, we explore the dynamics of crisis in sexual intimacy, the contradictions and confusions that originate in our culture, and the personal and social implications.

# Intimacy and Sex 7

*Sexual activity has a virtually infinite range of meanings and rewards.*

George Bach

The sexual expression of love is as personal and unique as every human born. When two totally different persons come together, their sensual complexities are greater than we can understand. Every time these two unique persons unite physically, each has a different experience, and each experience is different from the last. No matter how much we communicate about sex, we never seem to be able to capture what it is we experience or what it is we want.

Unconsciously, sex represents aggression for some and obligation for others, freedom for some and exploitation or oppression for others. The sexual expression of love varies from being a gift to being a weapon. Often, it is connected to winning approval. When the need to win or to be right becomes mixed with physical intimacy, sex becomes a conquest, challenge, or game. It becomes a competition to see how much, how many times, or with how many people we can play.

We have been taught that sex as a game or conquest is bad, and that sex as a gift is good. Since most of us want to see ourselves as good, we are sometimes troubled by the fun of sexual challenge or the satisfaction of seduction. We have been taught which motivations connected with sex are acceptable and which are not. In reality, motivations are multiple, complex, and often contradictory.

Sex often gets mixed up with power, which we are told is unacceptable. So complicated are sexual dynamics that we rarely uncover more than a few elements. To choose those sexual values that are most effective with one particular person at a specific time, we must consider what we have been taught.

## Sexual History

Every society imposes some limitations on sexual behavior to protect the group. Still, there resides in each of us some personal wisdom about sexual nature—a wisdom far deeper than we understand, something determined to endure regardless of social constraints.

To function, both society and the individual need structure and organization, which may take the form of social or personal conflicts about morality. Without some authentic framework, the breakdown of the community can occur. Social forces that tend to relate and unite people are weakened, as are personal forces that integrate the personality. We continually go through crises in our search for values to restore our personal and social integrity.

Evidence indicates goal-oriented societies tend to have strict sexual mores. In contrast, societies indifferent to or unsure of a direction are likely to be sexually permissive. Anthropologist J.D. Unwin, in *Sex and Culture,* says when compulsory continence, monogamy, and premarital chastity prevailed for several generations, these behaviors tended to produce great social energy, which became instrumental in advancing civilizations. He concludes that limiting sexual impulse and gratification creates more intellectual vigor in a society.

At the turn of this century, shocking the Victorian world, Freud published his theories on sexual instincts as our primary source of motivation. Although he used the term *sexual* in its broadest sense, the word was so loaded with emotional prohibitions that the public and scientific communities rejected both Freud and his work. Not until after World War I, in the 1920s, was Freud's work reassessed.

Freud called the sacrifice of instinctual pleasures sublimation. He said when sexual energy is diverted toward other ends, it becomes more socially valuable, resulting in "the common good." Similarly, historian Arnold J. Toynbee believed the later we postpone sexual consciousness, the better we can educate ourselves.

It often comes as a surprise when scholarly studies reveal that the real "sexual revolution" occurred *not* in the 1960s but after World War I. In the 1920s, premarital chastity began to lose its grip as the magistrate of morality. The introduction of the automobile, not the pill, hastened the death of Victorianism. It was the flapper, not the hippie, who discovered sex.

The next great shock wave occurred in the l950s with Dr. Alfred Kinsey's publication of a two-volume study that quantified sex. Kinsey, a biologist, and his researchers interviewed l6,000 men and women and then documented their sexual histories. He found that men are most active sexually from ages 15 to 30, whereas women are most active from 30 to 40. Kinsey observed that problems occur because men desire sex when women have not yet developed much interest in it. By the time women are interested, the responsiveness of the average man has diminished.

Kinsey forced us to look at the discrepancies between what we say is moral in sexual behavior and what we do. If all laws on the books pertaining to sex acts were enforced, Kinsey said, 90 percent of the American population would be in jail. Since Kinsey's reports, many laws have been passed to make previously illegal sex acts legal. However, despite the popular opinion that we Americans are sexually liberated, the chasm between our stated moral codes and our behavior is still vast.

For example, although prostitution, doing things we do not want to do in return for things we want, occurs in all phases of life—in work, marriage, and other situations—we discriminate only against sexual prostitution outside marriage.

In the l960s and 1970s, William Masters, a gynecologist, and Virginia Johnson, a psychologist, studied sex as a measurable physiological response. They documented what happens during orgasm. Through laboratory studies using volunteers, Masters and Johnson measured stages of sexual arousal for both men and women and found them to be the same. They measured orgasm in terms of time, intensity, and multiple orgasmic response.

Although some of their research findings are reported in this chapter, sex studies seldom shed light on our sexual feelings, attitudes, or thoughts. Scientists give us statistics on sexual expression without moral judgment. They do not delve into issues of quality like affection or love. Thus scientific studies of sex leave unexplained our most profound feelings and emotional responses.

From the puritanical obsessions of the past to the fascination with sexual skills today, we have been preoccupied with sex. According to psychiatrist Alexander Lowen, many people today are less sexually alive than those of earlier generations. He believes our level of sexual pleasure and fulfillment has decreased rather than increased.

Personal liberty is more vital to some persons than to others. For some, liberty is an expression of individuality; it is a personal condition, not a social one. For the young, liberty becomes self-creation, and social restrictions become servility. However, extreme sexual individualism may be incompatible with social survival.

Persons who value individual life satisfactions at the expense of society place sexual variety and pleasure high on their list of priorities. A social attitude that permits sexual latitude makes liberty possible. Paradoxically, this freedom is less likely to bring much pleasure. People tend to become bored or unhappy with their personal lives when free to choose among many alternatives.

Those who seek a sense of union with and commitment to others accompanied by deeply felt emotions tend to be more sexually discriminating. However, when their images of glorified sex fail to spiritualize the physical, they too become unhappy or confused. Except for brief moments, the ideal of love fails to live up to reality.

Romanticism attributes to sex greater meaning than it can bear. The hunger for spiritual satisfaction and meaning in life cannot be satisfied through sex. The glorification of sexuality actually inhibits those who experience disappointment, and they believe the fault lies in themselves.

Our ambiguous attitudes toward sex result in dualistic positions: love versus lust, physical versus emotional, private versus communal, spirit versus matter. When love fails to make sex less animal and more spiritual, we become confused. Lovemaking in the most heartfelt relationships can become casual and routine, but one-night stands can be brief spiritual connections. Casual sex and spiritual connections are not always mutually exclusive.

Socially defined sexual obligations offer a false security when externally imposed. *Responsibility* is the capacity to respond to and appreciate the self and other, to respect integrity in self and other, to hold oneself accountable for contributing to the emotional well-being of self and other. Personal responsibility, a uniquely human experience, can create a special kind of happiness through a sense of integrity and personal validity in a liberated society.

To accept sexual responsibility for personal choice at the expense of comfort in social rules requires that we continually reexamine and reshape our values. When we define ourselves by our potential for physical love, we must live with ambiguities, ambivalences, contradictions, confusion, and fear of failure.

## Sex and Guilt

Sexual experiences and attitudes are more closely connected to cultural prohibitions than to individual physiology. Eighty percent of 1,196 people in a survey said it is wrong for a man and woman to have sex before marriage. An even larger percentage believe monogamy is good and extramarital sex bad. At least on a verbal level, sex is prohibited.

Children learn early that sex is a taboo subject, that the body is connected to "don'ts," punishment, and shame. One man says, "I love my wife, but not sexually. She feels like a sister or pal to me more than a lover." The word *familiarity* comes from the same root as *family* and breeds a family feeling. The taboo prohibiting sex with family members can make some people uncomfortable with or uninterested in having sex with a "familiar" partner.

The attitude a person takes toward sex acts can make those actions positive or negative. If a person believes having sex with two people is promiscuous, that belief can result in a damaged self-image. When ideas of what is appropriate in human relationships result in guilt feelings, the acts become self-destructive. For example, "I am a bad person when I do this wrong thing" produces a negative self-evaluation that harms a person through self-inflicted wounds.

Self-definition is part of our sexual identity. For example, a person who believes good people are monogamous yet has fantasies about extramarital sex and gives them up earns the satisfaction and frustration of defining himself or herself as a good person. On the other hand, the adventurer who has a greater need for variety may enjoy identifying with being naughty by engaging in extramarital sex.

In certain religious groups, the males seek "good girls" for brides and then, for excitement and stimulation, spend their lives running after "bad girls." A double bind befalls sons who model their behavior after promiscuous fathers whom they hate for being unfaithful to their mothers. Some psychologists say in many intercourse experiences, six people are in bed: the two participants and the parents of both.

Although we try to control sexual mores through guilt, guilt feelings do not generally inhibit sexual behavior. In one study, 87 percent of the women and 58 percent of the men said they eventually accepted sexual activities that once made them feel guilty. Some—mostly males—said they had never felt guilty. The researchers concluded that people feel some guilt about their sexual behavior but continue their conduct until the guilt diminishes; then they move on to more advanced behavior and new guilt feelings until those too are conquered.

Although feelings of guilt and naughtiness interfere with the sexual pleasure of some people, doing what is forbidden increases the pleasure and excitement of others. Freud says sexual frustration is the basis for romantic passions, and if sex were free, men and women would have no need to idealize one another. Sexual tension makes us feel more alive, healthy, and attractive. The power of sexual tension lies in the acknowledgment of physical attraction accompanied by deliberate restraint. Vigorous sexual interest makes us extremely sensitive to being touched and stimulated. This tension is the magic and the passion that ends with gratification.

Some researchers study personality differences to explain sexual differences. For example, they find some people have a greater need for stimulation, excitement, and variety in every aspect of their lives. Evidence indicates people who tend to climb mountains, fly airplanes, hang-glide, parachute, and the like may also be risk takers in sexual experiences both in and out of marriage as part of their desire for variety and stimulation. Therefore, acting out the selfless devotion of mutual commitment and fidelity is a greater sacrifice for some than for others.

Sexual fulfillment is as elusive and undependable as every other aspect of love. Sexual expression varies with every incident. It is connected to personality, past experiences, and body chemistry. Although sex is only one aspect of intimacy, we often burden it with prodigious expectations, believing it will be our salvation. If sex is good, we believe our love will be satisfying and everlasting.

The paradox is that often our most wonderful sexual experiences, those in which we reach the greatest heights of ecstasy, occur with a person very different from ourselves, an incompatible person, someone we cannot live with. Fear of the unknown excites us as we are drawn to this different person with whom we cannot have permanence. The forbidden also attracts us, which makes extramarital affairs so exciting. Eventually, we learn that much of what we have been told about sex are lies, that sexual maturity is an obstacle course with booby traps along the way. Some consider this obstacle course a challenge and try to capture all the prizes; others tolerate it; and still others give up and withdraw. But most of us continue to believe some answers exist. We want to know as much as we can, for the subject of sex fascinates us.

## Gender Differences

Men and women, in general, have different sexual natures. For men, sex is often a single act performed in a brief period. For women, it tends to be a complicated sequence of events, beginning with attraction, seduction, and arousal, over a longer period. Biologically, a female's sexual nature begins with the sex act followed by conception, gestation, pregnancy, childbirth, lactation, and maternity. Generally, a woman's biological sex needs are different from a man's.

The role of society is to restrain unbridled biological tendencies. Social groups make laws to protect the weaker members by repressing the biological drives of the stronger. Thus, biologically, males compete for access to females, whereas females seek males who contribute maximally to their large investment in reproduction.

In her lifetime, a female produces a relatively small number of eggs compared to a male, who produces almost unlimited numbers of sperm. Moreover, women invest at least two years in the gestation and nursing of a single child; therefore, a woman is limited in the number of children she can have.

By contrast, a male can theoretically impregnate hundreds of females. Ismail, a 17th century king of Morocco is reported to have fathered 1,056 offspring. Although Western society does not tolerate such reproduction, these biological facts can help us understand why females who have a greater biological investment in the family tend to protect themselves from males. Biologists tell us sperm are cheap, and eggs are expensive. Thus females have a much greater stake in any one reproductive act.

Some sociologists suggest modern contraceptives and abortion have eliminated much of the biological female protective drive, leaving women as free as men to have indiscriminate sex. But most evidence indicates social changes do not affect biological drives within a short time span.

Margaret Mead suggests female protectiveness patterns occur cross-culturally. A Polynesian girl decides whether or not she will meet her "lover under the palm trees." In most cultures, the female has the final choice. A recent study of U.S. teenagers found that two thirds of the males but only one fifth of the females said sex was "all right with someone known only for a few hours." In West Germany, virgin 20-year-old women said they're "waiting for true love." Women are choosier, it seems, for evolutionary reasons.

Males and females also differ in brain organization and specialization. Girls speak sooner, have larger vocabularies, and are more verbal. Boys, in contrast, show visual superiority and excel in total body coordination. Boys also show more curiosity, hyperactivity, and aggressiveness. These differences, including hormonal ones, have been well documented.

Without reaching specific conclusions about gender differences, we know they contribute to confusion between males and females. A woman simply cannot experience what life is like inside a male body, and a man cannot imagine what life is like inside a female body. These sexual response barriers contribute to the crisis in intimacy.

One paradox rarely acknowledged is that, though most women's capacity for sexual intercourse is limited only by physical stamina, women can generally get along well without sex for years without any trauma. A woman's sexuality will not shrivel if unused. Intercourse may not be as important to many women, since women have three sources of intensely intimate or sexual experience: intercourse, birth, and breastfeeding.

A growing number of experts say what is sexually important to men may not be important to women, and vice versa. Dr. John Francis Steege, at Duke University Medical Center, maintains orgasm is not terribly important to some women. Although little physical difference exists between male and female orgasm, its *meaning* is different for men and women. As far as we know, in no other species of mammals do females experience orgasm. Male orgasm is necessary for reproduction, but female orgasm is not.

Physiological arousal for women seems to be a throbbing sensation, first throughout the pelvic region and then spreading throughout the body. For men, it is usually concentrated in the sex organ. For many women, this feeling of arousal is not just a stage on the road to orgasm but an end in itself. When the shift to intercourse comes, a woman's level of arousal may actually drop. Arousal is not merely physical for women. Feelings of affection and closeness to the partner are also usually involved. A woman wants sex with a person who loves and cares for her.

Finding fulfillment in physical intimacy over a long period may reduce the intensity of sex needs in both men and women. Because sex is readily available with a mate, some married persons say sex becomes less important over time. Single people who have experienced "instant intimacy" in many one-night stands say they no longer find fulfillment in free sex. Many people feel ambivalent about the whole subject. One young woman, when asked what she really wanted, answered, "Well, you see, I want it, and I don't want it."

Stories of liberated women and sexually confident men may be more make-believe than believable. Perhaps these people are found mainly in magazines and sex books rather than in everyday life. Books and articles on sex increase not only our expectations but also our stress in trying to live up to publicly defined standards that do not fit us personally.

Although there are gender differences, fear, guilt, and resentment affect men and women alike. They do more to damage sexual experiences than we can measure. A man or woman who, with compassion and caring, strives to alleviate a sex partner's fears contributes to making both the self and the other more fulfilled persons.

## It's All in Your Head

Dr. David Ruben claims that, in the sexual process, emotional feelings are more important than purely physical responses. He says sexual excitement is "99% in the head." Our "heads" have been programmed with socially approved and disapproved images of sexuality. Because these images are always changing, we experience confusion.

In the 1960s, we worked to eradicate repression and frigidity in females, vestiges from the Victorian era. We moved from sex is bad, dirty, and sinful to sex is good, clean, and healthy. More important, we were told sex is fun.

With the advent of "The New Morality," many Americans fought their way to sexual liberation. Sex manuals, like the *Joy of Sex*, were published by the hundreds. The demand was for orgasms or, even better, simultaneous orgasms. Information about the length of time before orgasm, frequency of sex, recovery time for males, and varieties of positions and techniques were graphically illustrated with photos and step-by-step diagrams.

As we supposedly became the most educated culture in the world on the subject of sex, our disenchantment grew. As a result, sex therapists set up shops to treat people with perceived sex problems. *The paradox is that with all of our education we have become more confused than ever.*

### The Way We're Supposed to Be

Sexual expression is of concern to society primarily because of its reproductive potential. Infants not wanted, cared for, or adequately socialized become a burden on others. For these reasons, we teach young adolescents, "Nice girls don't, and bad girls do." We tell young girls, "If you're really bad, you'll get caught and have an illegitimate baby, and your family will never live down the disgrace, and your life will be ruined." We tell boys, "If you get some girl pregnant, you'll have to marry her, you'll be financially responsible for paying all the bills and supporting two other people, and your life will be ruined."

Historically, disapproval has been somewhat effective in controlling behavior. Today, this kind of programming isn't working. In a recent survey, most Americans said it was immoral for teenagers to have sexual relations, and 70 percent disapproved of having children without marriage at any age. Yet in 1980, the number of white children born to unwed mothers reached one in ten, and almost one in every two black babies was born to an unwed mother. Almost one in five children were born to unwed mothers. Today, the proportion of these children is increasing.

In contrast to the guidelines about sexual morality we give young people, the mass media exploit sex. One women's magazine says,

The normal woman is sexual. She enjoys frequent feelings of sexual arousal and is not embarrassed to admit them. . . . She approaches lovemaking with joy and anticipation. And she is not reluctant to take the initiative in lovemaking.

Similar advice for men says good lovers perform with consummate skill and frequency, are knowledgeable about all sexual techniques, and can satisfy a woman to orgasm without fail. This tyranny of performance steers both men and women from great expectations to catastrophic disappointments.

At magazine racks, we find far more magazines for women than for men. Men's magazines specialize in sports and business, whereas women's magazines concentrate on advising women how to become perfect lovers, mates, wives, mothers.

* *The Ladies Home Journal*—"How to Keep Him Loving You Year after Year"
* *Mademoiselle*—"Exercises to Help You Rediscover and Develop Your Natural Sensuality"
* *Cosmopolitan*—"How to Improve Your Lover's Performance"
* *Redbook*—"Finding the Right Man"

Counselors and psychologists say women are far more willing than men to ask for help. Men find it difficult to be aware of or to admit their fears and anxieties. So women's magazines keep publishing advisory articles on sex for women who are then supposed to teach men. Paradoxically, reading these prescriptions often leaves readers feeling guilty, insecure, resentful, and confused.

### Contradictions

Pietropinto and Simenauer, in *Beyond the Male Myth*, report that of 4,000 American males surveyed, 61 percent said monogamous marriage was best. This figure is supported by a Harris survey in which 80 percent of Americans—men and women—believe in the commandment "Thou Shalt Not Commit Adultery."

In *The Hite Report*, 72 percent of husbands claimed to have had extramarital sex after only two years of marriage, which contrasts with a national survey that reported 60 percent of married men and 50 percent of married women claim to have had extramarital sex. In either case, the discrepancies between what we say and what we do are obvious.

Seventy-five percent of college students surveyed in 1986

said they expect to be happily married and sexually faithful. They also said they expect the divorce rate to continue to climb. These romantic illusions remind us how we tend to know what is true but think, "It's not going to happen to me."

In other ambivalent areas, both men and women have difficulty deciding who should be assertive. Women ask themselves, "How will he see me if I'm the one who makes the overtures?" Then they read in women's magazines, "Men like an aggressive woman." Some women decide to follow this advice by making advances even when they prefer being passive. Men say they fantasize about aggressive women, but most of them report they do *not* want their partners to be aggressive because it puts pressure on them to perform.

Both men and women say they prefer partners who are not jaded by having had quantities of sex partners, yet they are irritated by clumsy, inexperienced, coy, or inept partners. Most men want female partners to look sexually desirable, even subtly seductive so that other men will envy them, yet they become upset if their partner elicits sexual overtures from other males. A man wants a woman who knows how to please him, yet a woman who openly discusses sex or says she wants sex is often considered cheap or threatening.

Contradictions between our expressed desires and actual sexual behavior make most of us uneasy. Our own conflicts confuse us. One source of insecurity is that a woman can have sexual intercourse at any time and continue for long periods when she doesn't even want sex, whereas a man *cannot* have intercourse unless he has an erection, which he can neither will nor achieve on demand.

If a man does not have an erection, a woman may think she is sexually unattractive, and the man may fear something is sexually wrong with him. To defend their self-images both tend to place blame on the other. We either feel guilty because we have failed, or we feel resentment because our partner has failed. When our sexual experiences do not meet our expectations, we become disillusioned, resigned, or dissatisfied.

Most of us want to be knowledgeable and informed, so we read as much as we can about sex. Books and magazines give us norms, which are only generalities. Then we act as if they do or should apply to us. Statements such as "many men . . . " or "70% of women . . . " lead us to compare ourselves with surveys in magazines like *Playboy* and *Cosmopolitan*.

These magazines, along with current books on sexuality, use slanted survey samples. The people who respond to these surveys are hardly representative of the general population as a whole. Although percentages may imply neither good nor bad, they tend to set up criteria against which many people judge themselves as normal and healthy or abnormal and unhealthy. The errors in translation are not in the numbers but in our judgments. Finally, self-report surveys are suspect because they are full of self-deception if not outright lies. Often, the questions themselves are loaded, and the surveys flawed.

Besides comparing and judging ourselves, we sometimes try suggestions from experts. They list several erogenous zones supposed to have magical qualities but fail to tell us with what person, under what conditions, and when.

A man reads, "A woman will respond to stimulation of her ear lobes." When his partner acts irritated rather than stimulated, he feels rejected or inept. Then, in self-defense, he may say, "What's wrong with you? Other women like it." She, too, in self-defense, may either lash out at him or feel abnormal and at fault. Following prescriptions written by experts can lead to "cookbook" sex that lacks spontaneity and authenticity.

### Getting Synchronized

A major problem is frequency discrepancy—when two people in a relationship have different needs in terms of desire for sex. Those differences may be physiological, hormonal, or emotional. For two human beings to want sex in the same degree, at the same time, and for the same reasons is statistically impossible.

Biological cycles alone account for discrepancies. Just as people differ in their needs for food and sleep, so do they differ in their needs for sex. There are as many human variations as there are people. To be disappointed or to feel rejected when your partner does not want sex as much or as often as you do is as common as being annoyed if your partner wants it more than you do.

Along with biological frequency discrepancy, people differ in their emotional needs: wanting to be close, to be held, or to avoid loneliness. Sometimes busy schedules interfere. For example, a woman engineer who works alone all day lives with a man who, as a personnel manager, works with people all day. When he comes home, he wants some quiet time alone while she wants to talk and spend time together. These different needs cause hurt feelings and misunderstandings.

Our early teachings were to keep hands off things and people. As a result, some people are starved for emotional affection, whereas others dislike touching. A gentle touch can make one person recoil and give another person comfort.

A Purdue University study reveals that men and women interpret touching differently. When a woman touches a man, he considers the touch pleasant and indicative of warmth and affection. But when a man touches a woman, she often thinks all he wants is sex. What the initial touch may express changes with how it is received and with each experience.

When a man uses a particular kind of touch that is enjoyed by a woman, he tends to repeat that touch. Similarly, if she enjoys a certain stimuli, he will apply that same stimuli again. However, the freshness of the first time becomes stale with frequent use. Often, a touch enjoyed by a past partner may turn off a present partner. Or the kind of touching we like can be too gentle or too strong for the other person. When we use a touch or gesture that irritates someone, we tend to feel betrayed, misled, confused, or clumsy, as well as rejected.

Many experts claim that in lovemaking the partners should tell each other what pleases them. Sex therapists believe lack of communication is the major problem. But some people prefer a less direct approach. One person may interpret being told what is better as a complaint about present performance. Another person may prefer the subtle romance of nonverbal communication.

Since we have no control over others' perceptions, advice from experts often proves disappointing in practice. When we truly understand that what appeals to any particular person— what kinds of stimulation arouse or turn him or her off—is both uniquely personal and situational, we can stop taking responsibility for his or her sexual satisfaction.

What works once with a particular person may not work again. Each experience is different, and we are different each time. Physical loving is not isolated from emotional loving. We often do not know at any particular moment what we want. When we feel comfortable with ourselves, we relax, which lets our partners be comfortable with themselves and with us. Then we can be more free to sensitively explore the physical dynamics of the moment.

### Are There Any Facts?

A fact is *something said to be true or supposed to have happened.* Facts are simply publicly observed agreements dependent on language. First, we must agree on the meaning of the words we use. Then, to identify a fact, we must accept the same measuring system and the same definitions. A factual statement about sexual responses simply describes aspects of our experience, not the experience in its entirety.

Statistics are selected aspects that usually change drastically depending on how we define the terms and which parts of the whole we are measuring. They depend on what and how questions are asked, the biases of the researchers, and the validity of the population sample used.

---

Here is a list of facts compiled by sexologists. Ask yourself the following questions: Which of these statements, if any, apply to me or to my experiences? Under what conditions? When and with whom?

- Women ordinarily take much longer to respond to sexual stimulation than men.
- Men are more turned on by visual stimulation such as viewing nude female bodies.
- Sex drive in both men and women is partly caused by levels of testosterone, a male hormone found in both sexes.
- About 10 percent of impotence is caused by physical factors such as diabetes, obesity, alcohol, drugs, or high blood pressure.
- Apprehensions about performance; lack of affection or desire; feelings of hostility; and other attitudes, emotions, and beliefs account for 90 percent of all impotence.
- Women's orgasms vary in intensity far more than do men's as measured by heartbeat rates and vaginal contractions. Masters and Johnson's studies reported that women's orgasms measuring 3 to 5 contractions were mild, 5 to 8 were average, and 8 to 12 were intense.
- Recovery time for males after ejaculation and before another erection differs with the age of the man and the age of the relationship. The time is shorter in young men and in new relationships.

• Ten percent of women age 15 to 35 can expect to become unintentionally sterile by 1990—a consequence of sexually transmitted diseases.

---

Stating facts is one thing. Interpreting them is another. Like the rest of us, scientists often interpret facts to fit their own biases, assumptions, beliefs, and experiences.

Even well-read, educated, and experienced persons develop sex problems. Those who have read about the best lovemaking techniques or the most romantic gestures to use before, during, and after sex often have a tape running through their minds of devices to use to excite their partners. Their focus on a partner's performance is often perceived as a demand, which pressures the partner.

By reducing sex to mechanics, we lose our sense of humanity. Both parties end up feeling artificial, as if they were not personally involved in the experience. A sensitive person can tell when lovemaking follows a sex manual's formula.

These negative results from reading about sex are *not* in the reading. Sexual information is only more or less scientific. We can analyze studies, question results, and ask ourselves if the information fits us personally. All self-report surveys are suspect. We are not dealing with facts but human behavior, which may or may not be applicable to any particular person.

## The Swinging Pendulum

Historically, we moved from strict Victorian standards to free love in the 1960s. Beginning with problems of sexual repression and frigidity, we were told sexual freedom was the solution. So we read about whips and whipped cream, dating bars and hot tubs. We studied *The Joy of Sex*, with perfect performance as our ultimate goal. And we found that sexual freedom brought anguish and alienation.

Ideally, if we could approach each sexual encounter as if it were a wholly new experience, as if we were exploring this physical meeting of two unique human beings as something we have never before encountered, we could create opportunities for increased authenticity and vulnerability. Past experiences add as well as detract from present ones.

Social swings in values and attitudes affect each of us. The old double standard that allowed men greater sexual freedom has virtually disappeared. Since 1965, premarital sexual activity among men has increased 12 percent, whereas among women it has increased 35 percent. The new double standard, according to two sociologists, involves stated beliefs or values that contradict behavior. Young people say premarital intercourse is immoral and sinful, yet they engage in it. Men expect stricter morality from women, and women expect stricter morality from men. These sociologists found that members of conservative religious groups had stricter views on sex than members of liberal religious groups. *But when it came to actual sexual behavior, there was little difference between the groups.*

In discussing attitudes toward sex, young men hold more liberal attitudes than older men. Among occupational groups, professionals are most liberal, and farmers most conservative. Among geographical areas, the Western states are most liberal, followed by the North Atlantic, Eastern, and West Central states. The Southern states are most conservative.

These researchers found college-educated groups most liberal, whereas those who completed eighth grade or below were found most conservative. Thus age, sex, education, and geographical influences affect attitudes toward sex. The greater changes are in sexual attitude rather than in behavior. Changes in behavior lag years behind changes in attitude. Older generations find it more difficult to accept diversity in sex and marriage than to accept religious, political, or social changes.

Because of too much emphasis on the physical aspects of sex in the 1970s, many people today complain they have lost interest in sex. Among the many complex reasons for this loss of interest, fear lies at the center. Wardell Pomeroy, co-author of the Kinsey report, lists several of the most prevalent fears in males.

---

After reading the following two lists, one for males and one for females, list your own fears.

### Fears in Males

- Fear of being different
- Fear of impotence
- Fear of premature ejaculation

- Fear of being rejected
- Fear of inadequate penis size
- Fear of aging
- Fear of insatiable demands
- Fear of latent homosexuality
- Fear a mate will become sexually interested in other men

**Fears in Females**

- Fear of being different
- Fear of being frigid or unable to reach orgasm
- Fear of being left unsatisfied
- Fear of being rejected
- Fear of being physically unattractive or imperfect
- Fear of aging
- Fear of being unable to meet a partner's needs
- Fear of latent homosexuality
- Fear a mate will become sexually attracted to other women

---

Pomeroy's list of male fears is dated. Female fears, which he did *not* list, would include fear of pregnancy. Today, both men and women might list AIDS as their foremost fear. The fear of venereal disease has existed for centuries. A panel of doctors, including Dr. Helen Kaplan, director of the Human Sexuality Program at Cornell Medical Center in New York, claims that 50 percent of all married people have sex difficulties. The most common problem stated by them is a "lack of desire for sex."

Inhibited sexual desire (ISD) or asexuality is a process of not feeling sexual. It happens to happily married couples, chronic complainers, high achievers, loners, and lovers. Therapists estimate 30 percent of women and 20 percent of men who come to them for help are experiencing ISD. Helen Singer Kaplan, in *Disorders of Sexual Desire*, says there may have been as many or more of these people in the 1940s, but they just didn't admit it.

Young couples who are experiencing low sexual desire may have fewer than two sex encounters a month, and older couples may have fewer than two a year. These people often function well in life, look good, feel happy, like their families, and are successful at their jobs. Although low sexual desire may be natural for them, it often makes them feel something is wrong.

A movement of the early 1980s, "The New Chastity," stressed celibacy by choice. Some celibates recognized that the highest state of physical arousal occurred by postponing sexual intercourse. An article in *Glamour*, "Sexual Anorexia," suggests just as the food anorexic rejects food, the sexual anorexic rejects sex. More and more people graduate to rejection of sex as the solution to satiation, confusion, or fear.

Although by 1980, the spread of herpes and other communicable diseases had modified sexual behavior, by 1985, AIDS had become a terrifying, worldwide tragedy. Many people say they are unwilling to die for sex. And until scientists find a vaccine or cure, sexual behavior, as we have known it, will undergo enormous social and personal changes.

In *Male Sexuality*, Bernie Zilbergeld says, "Abstinence can be useful in many situations." When we want time to reevaluate our romantic involvements or sort out our values and feelings about sex, celibacy can be a relatively painless, gratifying experience. However, few young men voluntarily choose celibacy without wondering if there is something decidedly wrong with them. Today, as people give up sex rather than risk getting AIDS, they find abstinence isn't onerous.

We can offer our support to those who think a period of abstinence would be wise. Zilbergeld says, "And don't worry. No matter how long you stay in that state, you won't forget how to 'do it.' "

In our society, sex is big business. Magazines, movies, television, nightclubs, college campuses, automobiles, boats, beer, cigarettes, deodorants, shaving cream, mouthwash, and toothpaste are just a few of the products designed to sell sex. Although the sexual revolution as a mass movement affects us all, we can reject the hard sell and freely choose the most personally appropriate erotic behavior at any particular moment in our lives.

Now government is demanding that mass media give more time to health aspects of sex education. A recent debate in Congress emphasized the need for sex education as early as elementary schools. Moreover, the surgeon general recommends condom advertisements be shown on television. This health movement, initiated by the fear of AIDS, is worldwide.

## Sex and Love

People today seem to want a return to the personal virtues in erotic love. They want to keep the best of the reform movement without giving up love, spontaneity, commitment, and freedom.

Erotic love is a healing force that connects us with one another. All true lovers can join to celebrate the end of sex as an end in itself.

Sexual intimacy includes emotional, intellectual, and verbal components. We can love someone we do not respect or like. We can respect someone we do not love. We can have sex with someone we do not care for, and we can love someone without having sex with them. The ideal is to like, respect, care for, and have sex with the person we love, but in reality, at times, we resent and dislike those we love.

The Family Therapy Institute of the Western Psychiatric Institute and Clinic recently studied a group of 100 happily married couples who had survived the sexual liberating influences of the 1970s. These couples volunteered for this study after their marriages were rated as "very happy." Yet 90 percent of the people said they had a less than perfect sexual relationship. They reported a wide variety of sexual problems that they considered a normal part of marriage.

The most significant conclusion drawn by the researchers is *neither great sex nor any sex at all is crucial for a happy marriage.* Another conclusion is realistic expectations or none at all result in happier marriages.

Chastity, monogamy, and permanence in lifetime marriages provide social control. More effective contraception means sexual activity and sexual reproduction are no longer necessarily bound together. Two related changes—the desire for population control and the decline of the family as the primary socializing agency—have resulted in a new emphasis on the quality rather than the duration of relationships.

Although we have been preoccupied with sex, we derive little fulfillment from it when we use it as a substitute for other needs. As a means of aggression or rebellion or as a substitute for intimacy or self-value, the results are often dissatisfaction and emptiness. Sex by itself does not bring us peace. Eric Fromm says,

> An insecure person who has an intense need to prove his worth to himself . . . will be prone to think that the intensity of his desires is due to the demands of his body, while actually these are determined by his psychic needs.

Evidence indicates, paradoxically, with so much mass media attention to sex we are moving into an epoch of declining sexual behavior. Studies indicate societies with liberal attitudes toward sexual expression are likely to have less sexual behavior than societies that place sanctions on sex. More permissive attitudes result in less interest in sexual pursuits.

Sexual liberation imposes its own forms of bondage. The idea that sex is beneficial puts pressure on us to act out the standards set by the most liberated. Some social scientists say obsession with sex has drained the strength of the sexual drive so that it has become less important. For those who become sexually bored with their partners, after desperately trying every new position and every new avenue of sexual expression, finding new sex partners seldom solves the problem. The cure for sexual boredom is *to stop thinking about sex.*

The excitement of courtship and early sex simply cannot be biologically sustained. Sex experiences change with time, age, and partners. Some say the warmth and caring in a loving relationship are far more fulfilling than the sex.

The more fulfilled we are in other areas of our lives, the less likely we are to encumber sex with the baggage of unmet needs. When sex takes its place in the order of priorities with other interpersonal values, we experience a richer life.

Two people in a relationship can define and redefine what physical intimacy means to them. Instead of a synonym for intercourse, sex can mean physical closeness with or without intercourse, with or without orgasm, as long as the experience remains a source of sensual pleasure for both partners.

Sex is not a need to be fulfilled but a relationship to be explored. Although we will continue to find it difficult, at times, to sort out our own feelings about sex, men and women want the same things: shared contact, emotional support, and communication.

Even though love involves risks—the possibilities of pain, misunderstanding, rejection, or failure—most people want long-term relationships in which both partners commit themselves to exclusivity. Intimacy and closeness, most agree, are more important than orgasms.

To be in harmony with our varying sexual needs and expressions, we can acknowledge that each phase or stage, high or low, is transitory. We are travelers on our own roads passing through one place after another. We can enjoy change and freedom from fixed sexual identities and definitions.

Sexual unsureness is timeless and universal. Learning to

deal with helplessness means being willing to give and accept help from another person in a relationship. We can share our own sense of helplessness and experience moments of overcoming it.

We long for completeness, yet we must live with discontent and yearning. Every satisfaction reached ensures dissatisfaction will follow. Once we deeply experience another person in a relationship, a new demand arises to go beyond that place. Every time we successfully make contact and satisfy ourselves at one level, we extend ourselves, knowing we can be more and experience ourselves and others more deeply.

We will always be incomplete and unstable. We are never going to "get there," to that safe place where we can be forever protected. We must live with uncertainty, with the unknown in ourselves and in others, with the crisis in intimacy—that dangerous opportunity to go beyond where we are and to be more than we are.

# Intimacy and Resentment  8

*Intimacy . . . requires a type of relationship
which I call collaboration, by which I mean
clearly formulated adjustments of one's behavior
to the expressed needs of the other person in
the pursuit of increasingly identical, that is,
more and more mutual satisfactions.*

Harry Stack Sullivan

In the process of collaboration and adjustment for mutual satisfactions, each person in a relationship makes certain concessions, often giving something to gain something. At different times in our lives, we are more willing to compromise than at other times. And what we are willing to concede differs from one time to another.

Changes, such as wanting more or less closeness or privacy, occur so gradually at different stages in a relationship that we are seldom aware of them. To add to this complexity, we often want different kinds of intimacy—intellectual, physical, or emotional—at different times.

## Resentment and Guilt

Sometimes an unconscious anger at having made concessions, given up something we wanted, surfaces as resentment. *Resentment is a feeling of displeasure or indignation, a sense of having been insulted or injured by another.* In a relationship, if one person perceives himself or herself as consistently giving more than he or she receives, after some time, buried resentment often surfaces explosively.

The mother who wants to work but stays home to be "a loving mother," may eventually feel resentment. Even though the choice was hers, she pretends it is someone else's fault she didn't have a better life. Similarly, the husband who works hard and spends his time and money for his family, after many years, may feel intense resentment: "After all I did for them, and now they don't even care about me." Although this man chose the role of good, loving husband and father, he now feels injured and unappreciated.

The paradox is that if the mother had chosen to work instead of staying home and the father had chosen travel for himself instead of a college education for his son, they would feel guilt. Guilt tells us we chose our wants over others' wants. If we have an image of how a good mother or father should be and we fail to fulfill that image, we feel guilty. In contrast, resentment tells us we chose others' welfare over our own. Guilt and resentment are opposite sides of the same coin. Resentment is incrimination of the other, and guilt is incrimination of the self.

Today, married women who work say they do about 80 percent of the housework, cooking, and child care. In two-career marriages, men may agree to do their share but seldom actually do so. Part of the problem is that women often want their husbands to do the laundry or shopping just the way they, the wives, want it done. Another problem is that women see themselves as caretakers, especially of the family health and welfare.

Despite their own accountability for their negative feelings, women are more apt to experience resentment than men. To make matters worse, working mothers often experience guilt for not spending enough time with their children. Sometimes, guilt, resentment, or both are transformed into depression—a feeling of helplessness, of having no control over our own lives. But we can learn that we have control over our own lives and that we are, in fact, making choices.

All of us like to consider ourselves loving, giving, and unselfish. We also expect appreciation for our sacrifices. When a recipient of our goodness fails to fulfill our expectations and takes our generosity for granted, we tend to feel resentful. When we fail to fulfill our expectations of ourselves, we are more likely to experience guilt. Accepting ourselves with our human feelings of guilt and resentment helps us let go of such feelings.

Our experiences of guilt and resentment tell us we have freedom of choice. We are free to choose our own identities and to define our roles as we see fit—as good marital partner, good mother, or good father, for example.

---

Recognizing guilt as evidence of choosing to satisfy our own wants and resentment as evidence of choosing to satisfy others' wants can help us accept responsibility for our feelings.

- Recall a time when you felt resentment. What did you resent?
- Recall a time when you felt guilty. What did you feel guilty about?
- About whom did you feel these feelings?
- What expectations of yourself did you fail to fulfill?
- What expectations of the other person were unfulfilled?
- Do you sometimes use guilt for self-punishment?
- Do you sometimes use resentment to punish others?

---

Emotions such as guilt and resentment are much more complex than we understand. When we feel guilty or resentful, we are clinging to past roles and self-definitions. We experience the pain that accompanies loss—loss of an idealized or past self or an idealized or past role that no longer fits us. Looking back over our lives can help us find sources of these emotions, what triggers them, how we use them as habitual responses, what rewards we get from clinging to them, and how to let them go.

## Resentment as Separation

When we are 13 or 14 years old, most of us engage in an intense search for adulthood. We begin to wear adult clothes and use adult language. We want approval from others outside the family to reflect back to us an acceptable self-image. We know neither who we are nor who we want to be. Desperately, we seek the approval of others as flattering rather than factual mirrors.

*How* we associate with one another is more important than with whom we associate. If we lose a friend, parent, or partner who has given us acceptance, we feel as if we cannot go on without him or her. Separation from someone close to us feels like an irreplaceable loss. In this sense, dependent love is accompanied by a loss of identity, which in turn, results in resentment.

In our late teenage years, we begin our search for someone of the opposite sex who will find us attractive. We unconsciously agree to admire and flatter each other. Any honest criticism is regarded as a hostile attack. Since we are vulnerable to criticism at this time, we search for supportive others who find us acceptable. As lovers, we demonstrate how we would like to be treated. Love frees us temporarily from the isolation of not knowing who we are.

We form a mutual admiration society based on our need for association. Others help us define ourselves. Part of our self-definition comes from new roles in new relationships. If we feel happy, we believe our partner makes us feel happy. If our partner feels happy, we tend to take the credit; if he or she is unhappy, we think we are responsible.

In this process, we abandon responsibility for our own feelings, growth, changes, and self-definitions. Alone, we cannot be warm or kind or understanding. We need a recipient for our actions. Through them and how they are received by others, we define ourselves.

All actions have consequences. Repeated actions over a long period that fulfill past self-definitions may ultimately change from positive to negative. Actions appropriate in the past seldom satisfy us in the present.

Often we form a union with someone of the opposite sex to create a family. For many people, the desire to re-create the self through a child becomes a strong drive. Fear of death is sometimes overcome when we believe we can leave a part of ourselves alive when we die. We hope to make improvements by leaving children who are better than we. As we develop a new identity—good, loving parent—we become emotionally attached to qualities we project onto our children.

Insecure and longing for approval, we have children to love and admire us. Children are dependent on parents for physical and emotional support, so they both fear and resent parents, who in turn, love and resent them. Since fear, resentment, and hostility are unacceptable, we pretend they do not exist. Mutual dependencies include both love and resentment.

Dependent, young children admire parents who seem strong and capable. But in adolescence, parent worship turns to resentment as children learn their parents are false heroes. Parents then appear to be frauds, and children feel they have been conned. Children who adore their parents are more vulnerable than children who become aware of their parents' imperfections and weaknesses.

*Intimacy and resentment occur together.* Wanting freedom, each of us senses the other's need for our approval. Then we begin to experience the power that comes with independence. Fear of that power results in moments of scurrying back to dependent safety.

Paradoxically, as we become less dependent, we often give up resentment. Less dependent on one another for emotional acceptance, parents and adult children can learn to become friends. When we give up past self-definitions and role expectations to live in the present, we give up past emotions.

After many years of marriage, mutual pursuits and goals have been achieved. Children are gone. Though we welcome this new freedom, we also feel loss. A similar experience occurs when a person decides to retire from work. These transitions require that we redefine ourselves, explore new roles, and find new ways to use our time. Being confronted with choices at a fork in the road often brings a crisis in intimacy.

Although experts attempt to persuade us that intimacy is better than freedom, each of us must choose and periodically rechoose the degree of closeness or distance he or she wants. As we move into each new season of life, we do not consciously know the degrees (close or distant) or kinds (intellectual, emotional, or physical) of intimacy we want.

## Kinds of Intimacy

The person who develops self-esteem finds many sources of intimacy: intimate friends, lovers, siblings, classmates, or marriage partners. We can be intimate with others in many ways: intellectually, emotionally, physically, and so forth. Friends share intellectual or emotional closeness. Ideally, we are told, marriage partners share intellectual, emotional, and physical intimacy. However, many satisfying marriages do not include all kinds of intimacy, nor do different kinds of intimacy occur at any one time.

Intimacy needs rarely take the same form or are equally important to both partners in a marriage. At any particular moment, one partner has a greater desire for closeness than the other. Although, intimacy can be a time of intense sharing with someone we meet for the first time, it usually refers to the ongoing quality of a relationship in which an overall sense of togetherness is expressed as *we* as differentiated from *I* or *you*.

We want to know our partner in the deepest sense, in a union or bond that contains the other's presence even when we are separated. However, some people do *not* want to be known. In other cases, after many years together, a couple shares an identity. This shared identity may involve the paradox of "finding oneself in losing oneself in another."

Counterfeit intimacy may be expressed by the person who demands closeness for the purpose of manipulation or exploitation at the sacrifice of autonomy. Clinging-vine, compulsive-attachment closeness is often motivated by fear rather than by intimacy that thrives on differences. Exclusiveness or a mutual pact against the rest of the world may work for a while, but eventually, a mutual respect for the individuality and uniqueness of the partner is the foundation for real intimacy.

Whether this shared identity is an illusion or a choice of perception, real or imagined, is debatable. The real problem comes from expectations. To expect one relationship to always fulfill all the intimacy needs of both partners simultaneously is unrealistic. Most of us acknowledge that moments of closeness, warmth, openness, and trust interspersed with moments of distance, coldness, and even resentment make intimate relationships valuable and worth sustaining.

### Intellectual Intimacy

*Intellectual intimacy* includes words, ideas, roles, games, and language. When the intellectual needs of both persons are met, their communication interchanges can be fulfilling. For example, where one partner takes the role of teacher and the other takes the role of student, intellectual intimacy can be exciting. In each person's field of expertise, he or she can take the role of teacher. A couple also can be students together, researching a topic of interest and sharing information as they learn.

People are attracted to others for the way they think, for the mental stimulation and excitement they experience together. The couple that decides to go into business together often stimulate each other with creative ideas. They share financial goals and strive to achieve a common purpose. However, if one person in a relationship refuses to combine financial assets, mutual financial goals are absent. In many marriages, the partner most interested in financial planning takes responsibility for tax strategies, estate planning, insurance, and the many other business activities that lead to a secure, financial future.

*Intellectual intimacy is closeness resulting from sharing the world of ideas.* Sharing mind-stretching experiences—a book, television program, movie—often provides material for stimulating discussions. When there is a genuine touching of minds based on mutual respect for each other's intellectual capacities, intimacy is experienced.

Closeness often comes from sharing a broad range of activities involved in maintaining a house, raising a family, earning a living, or participating in community projects. Couples face common problems together. They join to support and strengthen each other and provide mutual stability.

In work-oriented activities, one person might build furniture while the other decorates a room. The mutuality that stems from work-oriented tasks brings many couples close and provides them with years of memories.

Some couples enjoy the same kinds of recreation—active or passive sports, camping, gardening, music, painting, and so on. They share the terminology of a particular interest. Similarly, a couple interested in travel might discuss geography or history; they accumulate a repertoire of experiences to draw from.

If these intellectual pursuits become unsatisfying, if one person wants to continue a particular activity, but the other tires of it, a conflict of interests may occur that requires compromise. For example, one person, fascinated with stamp collecting, can end up with a partner who resents that time-consuming pastime. Or a partner who goes camping or fishing to please the other, eventually feels resentful. Or the one who decides to give up a hobby because the partner isn't interested often plays, "If it weren't for him (or her), I could have been happy." People willing to give their partners space and time to pursue individual interests gain the rewards of space and time for themselves.

Couples who have a wide discrepancy in educational backgrounds or interests sometimes find intellectual intimacy unimportant in their relationships. For example, the person who works in a highly technical field, such as computer science or nuclear medicine, doesn't expect his or her partner to spend years studying so that they might share this specialty. In these cases, intellectual intimacy can be found with others at work.

Intellectual intimacy, although enjoyable, by itself will not make or break a marriage. When both partners are alert and interested in the world, in what is happening internationally as well as locally, they can contribute to each other's connections with the intellectual world while freely pursuing their own separate interests.

### Emotional Intimacy

*Emotional intimacy* involves the sharing of feelings; it is being deeply aware of those private yet significant perceptions of the other person—the touching of the innermost selves. Emotional intimacy, ideally, brings a couple into a common inner world of feelings. Each person empathizes with the other so deeply that they often perceive the outer world of reality in similar ways. Attuned to each other's emotional wavelengths, they sense what the other is feeling and, at times, know each other's thoughts.

Communication that facilitates emotional intimacy includes acceptance, disclosure, trust, confirmation, and interdependence. These ideals require expressing feelings in a safe environment, a place where one is accepted unconditionally and nonpossessively. In reality, the attainment and maintenance of emotional intimacy requires constant attention, time, and energy.

One-sided intimacy may be possible. In disclosing the self and trusting the other person, some closeness is experienced. If intimacy is one of my basic goals and I want to be closer than my partner wants to be, I can try to manipulate him or her into pleasing me, I can become resentful at not getting what I want, or I can allow my partner the privacy and separation he or she seeks. Still, the most satisfying moments of emotional intimacy are shared experiences in which both partners are involved.

The paradox is that once we achieve some level of intimacy, we often wish to move away into a space of our own. This skating back and forth between closeness and distance is rarely coordinated between two persons. At times, the conflict between our differing desires causes pain. Merely verbalizing our desires for closeness, with no strings attached and no demands for satisfaction, results in a release of tension.

Most of us can handle only limited amounts of emotional intimacy for short periods. Yet mutual caring and emotional understanding enrich our lives and our relationships.

In many relationships, the more needy partner's emotional giving often cannot be returned by the more private partner who has difficulty achieving the same degree of closeness. During much of the 24 hours when a couple goes about its daily routine—working, eating, sleeping—emotional intimacy is inappropriate. Disagreements or irritations often result in withholding intimacy, which in turn, results in resentment at not getting what one wants.

That anyone should want to avoid intimacy in marriage may seem strange, yet some people prefer the safety of emotional distance. Experts who say we fear intimacy often oversimplify a complex concept. A preference for distance does not necessarily imply fear. One man said,

I enjoy all the benefits of marriage: good food, clean house, clothes, having a child around. Sex, too. Yet I resent feeling tied down, restricted, responsible for others.

Emotional sharing requires self-disclosure. To reveal our innermost selves is often easier with strangers than with marriage partners. We may have too much invested in the marriage. Intimacy makes us vulnerable. Hurt, rejection, and disappointments experienced in marriage often leave scars.

Sometimes we find we are far more vulnerable than we want to be. One woman said, "I built up feelings of anger and resentment at him all along, from way back in the beginning. There were things he did that made me mad, but I never told him."

After years of marriage, some people give up their demands for emotional intimacy, and resentment fades. One 60-year-old woman said, "He fell asleep on me the night of our honeymoon. I didn't say anything, but I didn't forgive him for ten years. Now, I look back and see how silly I was."

One safeguard against vulnerability is to avoid the risk of self-disclosure by masking the true self. People become emotionally comfortable by playing well-defined roles. Doing and saying safe, expected things, we are saved from having to deal with real feelings and real people. It's far less taxing and leaves energy for other pursuits. The treadmill of life often runs more smoothly when we set up barriers to intimacy.

Once married, our priorities change. Often, we are unwilling to take the time to be intimate. Or, after years with another person, we assume we know who he or she is and what he or she thinks or feels. As we act out our roles, we lose touch with changing needs and feelings. Continually striving to accommodate or please a partner results in loss of self. When we act as the other person defines us or expects us to act, we give up personal growth and change for safety in sameness.

Men and women who have a poor opinion of themselves use the marital role as a convenient cloak to hide insecurities and weak self-images. One woman said, "I don't feel free to be myself because my husband wouldn't like me."

Pretense and deception may be better than open conflict and criticism. Emotional intimacy, at best, is experienced in moments of closeness followed by freedom. Those few persons who choose mates with compatible needs are most likely to find satisfaction in the relationship.

### Physical Intimacy

Physical intimacy begins with a friendly touch of a hand, a warm hug, a soft caress. It can be the same nonsexual touching we experienced in childhood. All physical touching, proximity, hugging, and caressing fit somewhere on the continuum of physical intimacy. We experience more physical intimacy as babies and small children than at any other time in our lives. Being held, rocked, fed, touched, dressed make up our first experiences of physical closeness. For some, the longing for physical closeness may stem from these early sensual experiences.

A man and woman may be close physically and still remain emotional strangers. Sexual intercourse is only a secondary definition of intimacy. Its primary meaning is a *close personal relationship that springs from the innermost self.*

The closeness that goes beyond sex manifests itself in many ways: eyes meeting across a room filled with people, a smile, a shared joke, a family ritual, a certain inflection of the voice, a spontaneous exchange of silent affection.

Longings for physical intimacy explain the dissatisfaction some people experience when they want physical closeness and end up with sex. Actually, expressing our love through our bodies may be easier than expressing it in other ways. Psychologist Rollo May says "the sharing of tastes, fantasies, dreams, hopes and fears seems to make people more shy and vulnerable than going to bed with each other." We often find it more difficult to share our deepest feelings than to share our bodies.

Sex leaves us confused when what we really want is to be held. Kissing, touching, and embracing that culminates in sex is often *not* what we want. We become unwilling to touch for fear of giving mixed messages and ending up with sex that leaves us empty. Of all the people asked why they stayed married for 40 or 50 years, not one mentioned sex.

Holding someone else feels like being held, which may partly explain the longing some women have to bear a child. The period when a baby is nursed, rocked, and held is often when many women feel most fulfilled. With children, we can touch without giving mixed messages, without sex as the end result.

Michael Morgenstern, in *How to Make Love to a Woman*, says, "Most women want romance—candles, compliments, flowers, dinners, little kindnesses and flatteries that can be offered and accepted without a return to old shattered sexual roles."

Morgenstern and his researchers interviewed 250 women to find out what it was that women really want. "This stuff is on people's minds," he says. "It's not just about sex and love and intimacy, but about the whole idea of people communicating."

Morgenstern says women are starved for attention and romance. They want their minds and hearts to be seduced first— tenderness and softness under the right circumstances and at the right time, an ambiance, a mood. He says it is better to err on the side of restraint than to push.

Men who take Morgenstern's advice and seduce women first for the ultimate reward of sex are being manipulative. Their caress comes across as a demand, which often produces resistance. However, some men resent the seduction game when what they want is sex. Most of us do not like having to pretend. Manipulation often originates with self-deception, with not knowing what we want or how to get it.

Physical intimacy requires a commitment to sensuality and physical affection. It includes the desire to relate, spend time with each other, give, achieve closeness, and discover new facets about each other. The careful nurturing of a relationship requires building foundations for mutuality and sharing. This intimacy demands attention and discipline; the cost is high.

Those rare moments when two people experience oneness are a complicated weave of emotional, physical, and spiritual intimacy. Although we long to repeat them, each exhilarating experience will never again be exactly the same. Those fleeting moments leave most of us wanting to re-create them. Like all peak experiences, they happen as if they have a will of their own, surprising us with their gifts.

## Seasons and Intimacy

The kind of intimacy experienced in the magical, passionate beginnings of a relationship differs greatly from the kind experienced in other periods. The life cycle of a marriage begins with the courting and engagement period—a time of passionate excitements and turbulent disappointments. The early years of marriage bring us face to face with reality.

As parents of preschoolers and then of school-age children, we move through other periods of the marriage cycle. Later, our children become adolescents and eventually leave home. Ultimately, we experience retirement and the death of one partner. In each phase of marriage, we bring unique and personal responses to crisis and intimacy.

Because of today's extended life span, and despite the higher divorce rate, the time that husbands and wives stay married, on the average, exceeds that of earlier generations. Thus marriages that end in divorce often represent the end of intimate associations that have reached points of diminishing returns.

When many of a couple's goals have been achieved— children are gone, financial security has been reached— adjustments in intimacy must be made. If two people have given each other many years of the best they have to offer, the adjustments and resentments begin to outweigh the advantages of their original collaboration.

For some couples, however, the last period of marriage may be the most peaceful. Time and trust bring acceptance of self and partner. They become true companions and value each other's imperfections. Companionship is more important to them than other values in life. Conversation or body contact may no longer be of any importance. Simply having the other person around can be comforting.

In contrast, after many years, some people want all those things they gave up during their marriages. They want what they didn't get or experience. Having limited their views and experiences to those connected with one other person, they find the narrow vision of marriage no longer tolerable.

The marriage was right in its time. Within the structure of marriage, many people feel they have inhibited their true potential to fit the needs of others. The separation, a time of crisis—a dangerous opportunity—becomes essential to personal survival. Endings, though painful, are part of every cycle and make room for a rebirth. Every relationship ends—some through divorce or separation, others through death.

## Intimacy and Being Single

In the United States, almost 70 million adults are single. The stigma against not being married is eroding. Today, it is not only acceptable to be single, but many married people wonder if the grass is greener on the other side of the fence.

One man in his 50s said,

I wanted to get married very much. Yet I resented her for losing my freedom. I was afraid to leave the security of marriage. This dependency made me even angrier. I didn't like the cowardly picture it presented. So I had affairs—escaping, but not escaping. Eventually, she divorced me.

Although some married persons fantasize about bachelor pads, swinging, and being free, until a real crisis occurs or their partner leaves them, they often stay with the status quo.

Singles International is an organization devoted to boosting the image and morale of unmarried people. Their Single Achievers Hall of Fame includes governors, mayors, famous entertainers, and sports stars. They plan conventions, have parties, and organize activities.

The either/or world—either you get married or you don't—belongs to the past. Today, we have multiple options. A few people will choose never to get married; some will marry when they are young; others will marry when they are older. Of those who marry, some will choose serial marriages, and some will stay married to one partner for life.

Many young people are taking more time to make a marriage commitment. Although some decide to live with a lover without the sanction of church or state, those that eventually marry the lovers they've lived with have the same separation rate as those who don't marry. Late marriages where both persons are close to 30 may have a better chance of lasting a lifetime because the span of time will be shorter, and they have experienced the freedom of single life.

Some young people who enjoy the company of the opposite sex want warm and friendly relationships with a variety of friends. They often enjoy their work and are unwilling to focus on a single companion. They like living alone, entertaining, and being free. Singles often do not want to assume responsibility for the emotional security of another person, nor do they want to become dependent. They want relationships that are free from obligation and that give them time to develop themselves, their careers, their future.

Similarly, some older people who have developed secure self-images, no longer need others as mirror images. As they develop their capacities for independence, they are less likely to be with others out of need or fear of being lonely. They live satisfying lives and make it clear to their friends that they are not looking for permanent relationships. They enjoy the opposite sex but do not want another person to be dependent on them.

They may be warm, affectionate people whose first priority is freedom. Often, they have fulfilled their needs to be married and to be good parents. They want to spend the rest of their lives without bonding, which to them, feels like bondage. For some people—for certain periods in their lives—nonpermanent, noncommittal relationships are satisfying. Solitude has become more companionable than it used to be.

Today, we have many more options than people had in the past. About 60 percent of divorced women and 75 percent of divorced men remarry and then divorce again. Serial monogamy, as demonstrated by the many marriages of Henry Fonda and Elizabeth Taylor, is common among those who feel they must legitimatize all of their love affairs. Making the commitment, they believe will ensure permanence.

We are less likely today to measure a successful marriage by the years it lasts than by the quality of it. Marriage for financial support, as an economic necessity, has faded with social welfare programs, two-career families, and economic affluence. A woman is less likely to stay in a marriage if she can support herself. One older woman said, "No person can feel secure if they can't make it on their own."

Emerson said, "For everything you have missed you gained something else; and for everything you gain, you lose something." Men and women who have fulfilled themselves with marriage and children have gained certain things at the expense of others. Likewise, those who do not marry have gained certain things at the expense of others. People who experience the companionship of marriage *and* the independence of single life realize the gains and losses of both lifestyles.

Some people who marry early and then divorce say middle age is a wonderful time to please themselves. After years of meeting the needs of others, being single is often a pleasant change. One woman said, "I get so much enjoyment from my own mind, I'm seldom lonely even though I'm often alone."

In the next several years, many singles will find a constant flow of people in and out of their lives. Brief encounters include significant moments; temporary alliances consciously made to give or get companionship, advice, and emotional support; short-term and long-term relationships to share both good and bad news, to call on someone in an emergency, and to enjoy a companion.

Some people mistakenly believe being single necessarily means being lonely. True loneliness is a basic sense of un-connectedness—the continued longing for the impossible in a union with another person and the unwillingness to accept one's own separateness. According to their own reports, adolescents suffer the most from loneliness, and people over 65 are less lonely than any other age group.

Those who choose never to marry have models like poet May Sarton who writes on "The Rewards of Living a Solitary Life." It is no longer a stigma but a viable option never to get married.

Many married people manage to get through the crisis of divorce, which has become a socially acceptable alternative. Support groups for divorced people exist all over the country.

Divorce and separation are painful. Men feel distress over sleeping alone, no prepared meals, an empty house. Still, after a while, they like having the time and energy to do things for themselves; they like the independence, the time to explore aspects of themselves that haven't been developed. After a divorce, adjusting to single life takes time.

There is a direct relationship between how long a person stays single and whether they will marry again. Most remarriages occur within two years of a divorce. The divorce rate is higher for remarriages than for first-time marriages. Those who become accustomed to single living, who stay single for five or more years, are less likely to marry again.

Death is another painful crisis. Since women live longer than men, most married women will become widows. Widows are less likely to remarry than divorcees. In *For the Woman Over 50,* Adele Nudelman says women over 50 no longer want to share the bathroom and kitchen. They don't want to fight over finances and sex. They enjoy not having to answer to anyone. One older widow says, "I like feeling complete. I like the unknown." Some women relish the new experience of feeling self-contained.

In a recent study of marital status among working women, single women had the lowest incidence of heart disease, even lower than married, working women, and suffered less from depression. Single men generally suffer more heart attacks and depression and die earlier.

Single life is more satisfying to the upper-middle class than any other group probably because they are financially independent. Describing his plans to close out a highly successful law practice, a 35-year-old lawyer said,

> I've spent my adult life accumulating money. Now I want to write. I plan to settle in Europe and see if I have any talent. If I were married, I could not break away. Some of my friends have children who are only a few years away from college. In their situations, they are not free to throw over a career.

Formerly married people who have gotten beyond the mad search for a soul mate and the compulsions of coupling find emotional support in family relationships, colleagues at work, friends, and lovers. Today, more people find periods between intense relationships can be satisfying. Meeting new people, developing new interests, or finding new work can be invigorating.

A supportive network helps people grow intellectually, spiritually, physically, and emotionally. Stimulation from a variety of different people can help us achieve our potential as human beings. We connect with different people in many different ways at different times and in different places. As a result, we find different facets of our own personalities come into play. A gift of time in a noncommittal relationship rarely is taken for granted as an obligation.

Some singles develop a "tender circle" of blood family and loyal friends. They are readily available in an emergency and offer understanding and emotional support. Others often have a few congenial comrades they see when they choose. With them, they can learn and enjoy activities. Singles also have infrequent contacts with people such as old school friends or distant relatives—the ones we all send Christmas letters to or phone once in a while.

Young people have the most need for affiliation—to be included in groups—but as we get older, we often want more depth in relationships with fewer people. We also want more time to ourselves to explore those personal activities best enjoyed alone. No longer do we need the constant support of others.

Today, when we can find people everywhere, we may simply want fewer people in our lives. After raising a family, many of us find it easier to find time for a small network of friends. We must regularly make decisions to balance quantity and quality in our relationships.

In our temporary alliances, we can give time, tenderness, caring, compassion, and kindness. We can do things for people when they are sick. We can clean a house, baby sit, bake a pie, or visit an elderly relative. We can help paint a room. We can cook and eat together. We are free to use our time as we wish.

In *Brief Encounters: How to Make the Most of Relationships That May Not Last Forever,* Emily Coleman and Betty Edwards write that many of us get "overpeopled." They suggest when priorities change, we can "unpeople." They suggest ways to achieve successful endings and caring closure. As relationships change, we can learn "good-bye skills," how to disengage.

With so many people, groups, and activities around us, we must learn to reorder our priorities, and then change them when they no longer work. Although people are interesting, we often enjoy them most *if* they do not take up too much of our lives. Along with a few deep relationships, we can have many uncomplicated encounters. Perhaps permanence is an illusion.

Stephen M. Johnson, in *First Person Singular: Living the Good Life Alone,* says autonomy requires certain skills: maintenance skills like cooking, housekeeping, and managing money; communication skills like initiating conversations and meeting new people; and social skills like making and maintaining friendships.

Johnson says at different ages we need different things. After years of caring for family, we can now find interest and pleasure in community goals. We can care for strangers. Autonomy, he says, doesn't mean not caring. Within a caring network, we can give up what we have been for what we can become. He suggests we pay attention to balancing mental, physical, emotional, social, and economic needs.

Divorced people can plan holidays together and organize activities. One single lady is known for her "Christmas Dinner for Strays," an annual event for her circle of friends. Everyone brings their favorite dishes for the dinner, and all of their children participate. They have yet to experience the kinds of hurt feelings or conflicts that sometimes occur in blood families.

As singles, we must learn new ways of being. Unlike a chair or table, which is defined before its existence, human beings exist first and then create their own essence, which is constantly being created and re-created without ever being perfected.

It isn't that being single is better than being married or that being married is better than being single; the key issue is that we choose and rechoose every day of our lives from all the possibilities. Most of our decisions are not irreversible.

Given the person you are today, the situation you are in, all of your past experiences, and all the information you have, you are probably making the best decision for yourself at this time in your life. Once you have made a decision, you have more information to make a later one.

If we are growing, changing persons, our decisions will change. Those of us who have had a compatible marriage and been fulfilled with what marriage has to offer may choose to be single. If or when we reach a point of diminishing returns with being single, we can choose another way of living. Because of the pluralistic nature of our society and the complexities of the human personality, we, over a lifetime, choose and rechoose daily—even when we stay with the same person for life.

In our culture, marriage will probably continue to be the preferred choice for meeting intimacy needs. Among long-lasting marriages, 20 percent of the couples say their marriages are ideal. Another 20 percent say they lead "lives of quiet desperation." The remaining 60 percent lie between these extremes.

Some people see their lives as a glass half full; others see their lives as a glass half empty. All of us create our own visions of satisfaction and resentment as the foundations of living through the many crises in intimacy that occur in our lives.

Resentment, hostility, guilt, and negative feelings are as much a part of intimacy as love, affection, and positive feelings. Each of us chooses certain attitudes toward life that are inside us and unconnected to being married or single. Some people live a lifetime without finding satisfaction in anything. Others create satisfaction in both relationships and work. In the next chapter, we explore the satisfactions people find in their work.

# Intimacy and Work 9

*Blessed is he who has found his work; let him ask no other blessedness.*

Thomas Carlyle

S cientists are unable to distinguish all the characteristics of humans from those of other animals. However, many social scientists agree that among those activities most peculiar to humans, work probably defines man with the greatest certainty. We seldom understand the nature of our most *intimate needs*. Not knowing the innermost character of ourselves, we can lose touch with the fact that work is essential and fundamental in our lives.

Few books deal with *work, the way we make a living*. We tend to favor the fiction that whom we go to bed with is more important than what we get up for in the morning. Even biographies and autobiographies often slight the subject of work. People actively involved in their work tend to have initiative, creativity, and satisfaction in their lives.

Freud said all humans have two great capacities: to love and to work. He said some of us sublimate our life energies into long-term projects hoping to gain recognition, and some of us displace a need for recognition through work with an insatiable hunger to be loved.

These two drives—work and love—seem, at times, to be antithetical. Francis Bacon, in his essay "Of Marriage and Single Life," wrote,

> He that hath wife and children hath given hostages to fortune; for they are impediments to great enterprises. . . . The best works . . . have proceeded from unmarried or childless men.

We might add, "men and women." However, Bacon's statement may or may not be true today.

The saying that women live for love, and men for work may no longer be accurate. A nationwide Harris poll asked women,

> If you had enough money to live as comfortably as you'd like, would you prefer to work full time, part time, do volunteer-type work, or work at home caring for the family?

Only 28 percent of working women wanted to stay home. Women, as well as men, want to work. The unhappiest women today, those reporting more depression and poor self-esteem, are nonworking and married. Although professional workers tend to be happier than nonprofessional, men and women alike say they value work.

---

People give the following reasons for working. Which of these values is most important to you?

- To sustain physical life; for food, shelter, and so on
- To provide a sense of reality (identity)
- To contribute to self-esteem and self-worth
- To measure achievement or status
- To improve my material world; as an economic function
- To produce something of value
- To fulfill a social purpose; for connection with others
- To achieve a sense of fulfillment; as a measure of worth
- To impose order or structure on my world
- To control space and time patterns and rhythms

What other reasons would you add to this list? Over time, the order of importance may change as you change.

---

Most of us yearn for work that is meaningful, expresses our unique creativity, and adds positiveness to our personal lives and to the world at large. Ironically, the two basic human social arrangements—family life and work—provide us with possibilities for both great frustration and great satisfaction at the same time they may interfere with each other. Still, some people, over a lifetime, "have it all."

The normal patterns of our lives are not conducive to uncomplicated satisfactions. We are only dimly aware of our drive for activity. When children get too active, they irritate us, and we tell them to sit still. Needs for self-expression, self-realization, and meaningful activity are often denied.

We have talked about the human need for an accurate and acceptable self-image that needs to be verified and expanded through associations with others. An equally strong drive is *to verify and expand the self-image through action*. Those who like their work usually like themselves.

Perhaps the most damaging form of personal rejection is to deny a person something useful to do. For many of us, being without work means being without worth. When unemployment rises, we experience troublesome forebodings. We understand the anguish of the jobless. Albert Camus said, "Without work all life goes rotten." Many of us tend to define ourselves and others by what we do. Our work not only provides us with satisfaction but also with a sense of identity and worth. When asked about the value of work, one woman said,

> Through work I support my existence and personal autonomy. Work gives my life shape and enriches me. I experience the pleasure of developing my human powers.

## The Value of Work

The human need for diverse physical and mental activity leads us to experience our many capacities and to become more intimate with the deeper levels of ourselves and others. Potentially, we can find almost any activity rewarding. People financially able to live without working are often conscious of their need for purposeful activities. When senior citizens fought for the right to continue to work, we outlawed mandatory retirement. Americans consider work an inalienable right.

Yet many Americans have ambivalent attitudes toward work. Since we do not expect or understand ambivalence, we often deny work drives simply because we cannot imagine having them. We are likely to alienate our interest in doing things we label "work," which unfortunately, includes most of our activities. The Greeks thought work was degrading and gave tasks like doing the laundry to the underclass. Whether an activity is work or play depends on both personal and social values. Work for one person—gardening, rebuilding an old automobile, carpentry, fishing—is recreation for another.

Eighty percent of Americans say they would continue to work if they inherited enough money to live comfortably without working. Seventy-five percent of Americans say they are satisfied with their jobs. However, when asked whether they would choose the same kind of work if they had their lives to live over, only 43 percent of white-collar workers and 24 percent of blue-collar workers said they would.

Although work plays an important role in the lives of most Americans, a major study indicates increasing discontent with work. Among American workers, alienation is widespread. Alienation, a feeling of separation from one's society or group, involves perceptions of one's work role as meaningless and of oneself as powerless. *Alienation occurs when people feel they have no control over their lives and are detached from their own activities and the people around them.*

Today, people want quality in their work life. They are more concerned with their potential for growth. They want jobs to be less depersonalized and more interesting. Most people seek better paying jobs with more challenge, satisfaction, or status.

### Historical Changes in Work

At the beginning of this century, most men worked a 12-hour day 6 days a week. After World War I, we Americans were proud to reduce the work day to eight hours and the work week to five days. Twenty-five years ago, a good many workers tolerated unpleasant job conditions for economic security. The foreman's job was to assign work and tell workers what to do. He judged performance and fired those who didn't perform well.

Many workers raised by immigrant parents toiled to give their children a better life. They learned that work was a driving force connected to dignity and hope. These people didn't ask questions about work. They believed it was a necessary part of living and considered unemployment a tragedy.

A generation ago, a working man, "the bread winner," provided the sole financial support for his family. They depended on him. Most men simply accepted their responsibilities, even if their work wasn't as stimulating as they would have liked. But after World War II, the Puritan ethic of hard work, regardless of working conditions, declined as women entered the work force.

In the 1950s, we experienced a period of economic affluence. The Great Society brought with it social welfare, food stamps, free medical care, unemployment insurance, and social security. Some people were no longer willing to work at disagreeable tasks. If they couldn't make more money working at something they enjoyed, staying home on some form of government aid became preferable. But as government subsidies increased, so did unemployment and despair.

After World War II, 50 percent of men over age 65 worked. Today, less than l9 percent work. Three out of ten men 55 to 65 are no longer working, and among the less educated, fully 50 percent are unemployed. Thousands of women now earn more than their husbands—not because their incomes are high but because many of their husbands are unemployed or employed only part time. Some draw unemployment insurance, disability insurance, or social security. In families having two or more incomes, no one person is essential to the family's economic security. As more women went to work, the number of men who dropped out of the work force increased dramatically.

Workers today want a new set of job satisfactions. They dislike authority, hierarchical relationships, and having a boss that tells them what to do and has the power to fire them. They dislike routine. They want variety, interesting work that pays well. Above all, they want personal recognition for what they do.

Individual productivity declines in group situations. For example, a German psychologist, Walther Moede, reported results of group performance on a rope-pulling test. He found that three people pulled as hard as two and one-half individuals, and eight people pulled less hard than four individuals.

In 1974, a group of researchers at the University of Massachusetts repeated this experiment by blindfolding participants and telling them others were pulling with them when actually they were pulling alone. People pulled at 90 percent of their ability when they thought one other person was pulling with them and at 85 percent when they thought two to six others were pulling.

Other researchers who have set up different kinds of tasks, such as clapping and cheering together, consistently find that the sound pressure generated per person decreases as group size increases. The experimenters called this "social loafing." Perhaps feeling credit is divided in a group regardless of individual contribution makes people less willing to work in team situations. Ultimately, the value of work as self-fulfillment may come from the recognition of individual accomplishment.

In the United States during the 1970s, our productivity level began to fall below that of some other industrial countries. Low productivity, poor quality, foreign competition along with an economic recession and high interest rates contributed to high unemployment. Today, those conditions are changing. In the 1980s, many American products improved and can now compete with the higher-quality work found in foreign products.

In 1982, unemployment edged up toward 11 percent. Cuts in welfare programs sent many people searching for jobs. For the first time since the Great Depression, many Americans who had worked all of their adult lives in industries like steel, housing, and autos were laid off.

During most of 1983, newspapers trumpeted the news that employment was increasing and unemployment rates were dropping. However, almost 10 million people, 8.2 percent, remained out of work. Although the unemployment rate today continues to decline, we still consider unemployment intolerable. The trauma of not working leaves emotional scars. The news media coverage of people without work affects those who do work. When unemployment is high, workers are less likely to ask for raises in pay or more benefits.

Today, with a lowered inflation rate, the old battle cry for more money has subsided. The general attitude is that those with jobs are fortunate. With lowered unemployment, a low inflation rate, and low interest rates, the economy in 1987 appears to have improved. Most economists feel generally positive about the economic balance of the near future.

However, many workers say security is not enough. People today demand more from their jobs. They want more autonomy. Workers say where they lack control, they lack responsibility. Pride in a job well done for the sake of doing it well may be a value of the past, but disenchantment with work is not a new phenomenon. Questioning people will not accept work as a duty or spend their lives working at something they dislike. Young people are less willing to live without thinking, do what they are told, or work without choice. If a person spends 100,000 hours of his or her life working over a 50-year life span, choosing how to spend that time is important.

A new movement called Right Livelihood concerns itself with work that harmonizes with well-being, gives workers a sense of fulfillment and completeness, and corresponds to the workers personal satisfactions in life. The concept of quality circles is a yearning in people to be used well and to use themselves well. Industry has learned people want to produce something meaningful to themselves.

Today's workers have high expectations. If their jobs are mechanical, boring, repetitive, or dreary, they complain. When workers find they are in dead-end jobs with little responsibility and poor growth prospects, they become increasingly dissatisfied.

It is not uncommon for employers to offer good workers a raise to keep them. Yet according to the National Association of Personnel Consultants, eight of ten people who accept a raise leave their jobs within six months. Employers complain, "Nobody wants to give a good day's work for a good day's pay." And members of the older generation sadly say, "The work ethic and pride in doing a good job has died, and nothing better has taken its place." Many people do not know what they want from work.

---

Ask yourself the following questions:

• What are you looking for in a position?
• What role does money play?
• What scope of responsibility do you want?
• What kinds of relationships do you want with bosses?
• Are you ambitious enough to balance a job with more education or a degree?

---

The qualities people value in a marriage—permanence, commitment, security, loyalty—are the qualities employers value. Sometimes an employer views employee dissatisfaction as disloyalty. In a tough economy like today's, a boss may offer a disgruntled employee a raise to buy time to get a replacement. However, research indicates unhappy employees often do not have money on their minds. They want recognition, responsibility, or the possibilities for advancement.

Executive search firms say loyalty is no longer relevant in the work world. Raiding companies is common and turnover is high, particularly with executives earning $60,000 or more a year. In some cases, a worker's loyalty is no longer to a company but to a professional group—doctors, lawyers, educators, and others.

Although job dissatisfaction is a complex subject, we can ask ourselves how to increase our satisfaction at our present jobs before searching for greener pastures. Our choices in work create the same kinds of ambivalence as the lifestyle options of being married or single.

Many people actually turn the little things they dislike about their jobs into monsters by putting off doing them or taking care of them when they're tired or irritated. By rearranging time, refueling at lunch time, and saving enjoyable projects for the end of the day, work can become more pleasurable.

Those who say if they had their working lives to begin again, they would choose another line of work often do not take the initiative to make a change. Most people fall into their jobs rather than deliberately choose them. In a recent Gallup poll, 84 percent of Americans report they feel some pride in their work. For most people, making changes takes too much effort.

Some of our job-related unhappiness may be tied to internal changes similar to those occurring in other relationships. A person's age often plays a significant role in job dissatisfaction. At age 30, a critical stage, many of us reappraise the kind of life structure we built in our 20s, including the work we do. The most dramatic time of unhappiness with work comes at around age 40. Today, many of us are ready to move on and find a different profession.

Like serial monogamy, job satisfaction requires different things at different stages of life. However, recent studies indicate the older a worker becomes, the happier with work he or she becomes; the more job satisfaction a person achieves, the longer he or she lives. Anxiety and responsibility accompany freedom of choice. Our world today is complex and requires new, creative ways of making work an important and intimate part of our lives.

### Changing Conditions at Work

Today, employers express a broader concern with worker satisfaction. Some corporations have introduced counseling to replace the rules and penalties of the past. Some hire outside consultants to run climate surveys and set up grievance systems for handling complaints. Employees can anonymously express their opinions about pay, promotions, and job discontentment. The goal is to boost worker morale and productivity.

Regular round table meetings involve both managers and employees who are included in decision making. Although some workers abuse these new systems and some managers or supervisors can't handle giving up control, overall, the results have been positive. Improved morale, decreased absenteeism, less turnover, and fewer grievances have resulted. Career counselors explain salary and promotion options. They take office opinion surveys and explain workers' rights to appeal. They recognize the team concept—each person's views are important, each has something to contribute. Workers want a voice in decisions that affect them.

New approaches include work teams that negotiate among themselves, setting up schedules and talking out problems. The self-management concept represents a wave of change in factories. Self-management means a subordinate will sooner or later make a bad decision, but managers must give up control and live with the mistakes. Still, where self-management includes setting goals and arranging the work environment, workers experience less alienation and more internal rewards.

Work and education are merging. Many corporations have on-the-job training and education. New workers attend orientation meetings before starting the job. Workers are given time off to attend classes at local colleges that give credits and degrees. Many students get credit for work experience.

Another important trend is that many firms find they can make more money when their workers own stock. People work harder, more creatively, and more efficiently if they own a part of the company. Employee ownership is one of the fastest growing trends in American business. In 1976, 300 U.S. companies offered employees some kind of ownership plan; in 1982, more than 5,000 did.

In 1970, Congress enacted legislation giving companies significant tax advantages for offering employees equity. Companies can deduct contributions from taxes. Several government agencies also offer loans to assist employee ownership. Research studies indicate employee ownership results in greater productivity and more profit.

A Senate survey found that firms averaged a 155 percent increase in profits in three years after instituting employee ownership. Among these firms, a University of Iowa study showed a productivity increase of 78 percent while comparable conventional firms showed a productivity decrease of 74 percent. This kind of research is only one measure of how work conditions are changing.

When workers have some control, are involved in making decisions or running the company, and are utilized productively, they find more satisfaction in their work. Human beings need to feel they are doing something important or exciting, that they are making a difference. Work lends dignity and purpose to life.

### Love of Work

So often do we hear complaints about work that a person who loves to work is labeled a workaholic and thought to be abnormal or a problem to his or her family. Psychologist Marilyn Machlowitz researched people who love to work. In her book *Workaholics: Living with Them, Working with Them,* she concluded that work fiends are often happy and emotionally healthy.

The love of work begins in the early years. The child who hates to take a nap, doesn't have to be told to do schoolwork, and takes on extra projects may grow up to be a workaholic with a zest for work that spills over into other areas of life.

A common trait of work-lovers is they tend to do more than one thing at a time. They shave while driving to work, take business to the bathroom or beach, read magazines while glancing at television, learn a foreign language by cassette while driving to work, talk on the phone while writing a memo. Functional things like meals and housekeeping are done rapidly. They want to beat the clock, use seconds other people don't notice. They want to live two lives for the price of one.

No matter how late they go to bed, they get up early. Their work is their leisure. Rarely do they feel overworked. If they have a job that lacks challenge, they find something more exciting to do. They have a lot of confidence because they seldom fail at anything they do. Paradoxically, fear of failure keeps them from failing. Often perfectionists, they use lists, appointment books, and time-saving devices that enable them to master every minute. In addition, they usually have an abundance of energy, drive, efficiency, enjoyment, and enthusiasm.

Few family members are pleased that workaholics are lucky enough to love what they do for a living. Family members often become upset because they feel the worker may be staying away to avoid being with them. Work-lovers do not work primarily for money or status but for the joy and pursuit of accomplishment. They do not need as much social approval as others. They say they are less lonely than people who do not enjoy their work. A love of work is often related to enjoying life.

However, we often feel embarrassed to say we love our work. Complaining about work sometimes creates feelings of sympathy in others, whereas saying we enjoy work more often creates feelings of envy or guilt. As a society, we tend to believe anyone dedicated to his or her work is somehow weird, a threat to our own self-image, especially if we do not enjoy our work.

Faced with someone who loves his or her work, people often rationalize their own dissatisfaction with work by making the work-lover wrong. Even some therapists and psychologists perpetuate this negative labeling when they suggest something is wrong if life is not balanced equally among relationships, work, and leisure.

Old friends and relatives often withdraw because a work-lover reminds them of what they haven't accomplished. They feel resentful, jealous, or inferior when around a successful person. But successful people seldom let negative feelings about their being workaholics bother them. Actually, envy shows others wish they enjoyed their work.

At any given time in life, a person may make deep commitments to work, followed by commitments to personal relationships. Total commitment to the joys of work and the joys of relationships at the same time may not be productive, especially if one's work is science, research, or writing. The commitment of time when divided among many interests may dilute them. Some fortunate people in the helping professions find in work satisfying relationships as well as the freedom to do what they like.

An optimal performer, on the other hand, has a passionate commitment to work but also knows how to relax, delegate authority, and surround himself or herself with competent people. The optimal performer sets goals and improves communication. The work-lover knows his or her own needs; is intimately aware of unique, personal abilities; and is involved in the pursuit of excellence, which leads to finding satisfaction in life.

### Being in Control

A comedian once remarked,

> Freedom is being able to do what you please without considering
> anyone except your wife, the police, your boss, your life insurance
> company, your doctor, your airline, internal revenue, state au-
> thorities, and your neighbors.

Feeling free is an experience of being in control of one's life,
of being able to choose one's actions. Frequently, we do not want
to be where we are or to do what we are doing, but we generally
accept these moments as transient. People who feel constrained
feel as if their actions are subject to punishment by external
forces over which they have no control.

To study the effects of feeling in control, two researchers at
the University of Chicago used a technique called the Experiential Sampling Method. Giving a group of volunteers
electronic pagers to wear, the researchers collected more than
4,700 self-reports of everyday events.

Each time they activated the beeper, the volunteers were
asked to fill out a page in a booklet indicating where they were,
what they were thinking about, how they felt, and to what
degree they would prefer to be doing something else. This sample of rather typical Americans showed white-collar workers
generally feel freer than blue-collar workers and, in most situations, men feel freer than women. When they are doing what
they want, people feel free and happy.

One question, "Why were you doing this activity?" had a
choice of answers: "I had to," "I wanted to," or "I had nothing
else to do." Fifty-one percent of the time, people said they felt
free and were doing what they wanted to do. While at work, only
15 percent of the responses were "I wanted to." While traveling
or house cleaning, 35 percent of the responses were "I wanted
to."

People said they felt most free when engaged in leisure activities like socializing and watching television. Although the
women socialized more and had more leisure time (worked less)
than the men, they felt free only 47 percent of the time, whereas
men rated themselves free 53 percent of the time. Women spend
considerably more time in personal care and feel "they have to"
do it. Women also reported feeling less free at work.

On a scale of 0 to 10, people rated themselves most cheerful
when they were doing what they wanted. A sense of personal

freedom is experienced most often by people satisfied with their lives. The researchers concluded that many of our actions need not be felt involuntary. Part of the time, for some persons, even compulsory activities are experienced as free. For example, some workers enjoyed their seemingly routine assembly-line tasks.

Although enjoyment of repetitive tasks is unusual, attitude may be more significant than external circumstances. When people feel their activities are freely chosen, they are more cheerful and more involved in what they're doing.

The researchers concluded by saying, "To some extent, the experience of freedom is independent of outside conditions." Some people feel free even when conditions seem to deny its possibility, whereas others feel a lack of freedom even under the best conditions. This discrepancy between objective and subjective realities seems intimately related to attitude.

## Attitude and Work

*An attitude is an enduring system of positive or negative evaluations, feelings, and tendencies toward certain actions or behavior.* Attitudes affect what we learn and remember, what we perceive, and what we do. They determine the enjoyment we get from work, the ways we handle money, and how we feel about our lives. We develop favorable attitudes toward whatever meets our needs and unfavorable attitudes toward whatever thwarts or punishes us. Attitudes influence our relationships at work and the activities we engage in.

To some degree, children learn attitudes from adult models. Parents who talk about "Blue Monday" and sigh with relief as they say, "Thank God it's Friday" teach children that work is unpleasant, something they "have to do" to earn a living, to get a paycheck, to live. However, as adults, we can select our own attitudes and direct our own behavior. We have some free choices about our thoughts, attitudes, and actions. Positive attitudes radiate energy and success; negative attitudes breed unhappiness and fatigue.

Optimistic people are generally more positive and view life favorably. Pessimistic people are generally more negative and view life unfavorably. We are not positive or negative in all situations. A positive person at work can be a relatively negative person at home. But if a person is unhappy at work, that negativeness will probably spill over into relationships outside work.

One element of worker dissatisfaction comes from the attitude of being a victim. The victim mentality takes the position, "I am a victim of outside forces." A victim blames lack of education or job skills on personal history, genes, family, social class, parents, or teachers. Dissatisfaction with work, a victim blames on a lack of opportunities and on targets like the boss, the economy, the times, the corporation, technology, and government.

The attitude taken by the victim is that of being powerless. Usually, a victim position is one in which there is a deep belief in the right to be taken care of. The right to work, for some Americans, has become the right to free income without working or to income *beyond contributions* to unemployment insurance or social security.

A person's attitude toward work affects other areas of his or her life. For example, a school custodian who recently retired after 40 years of working with teachers and students said, "My work was important. The children and the teachers appreciated what I did." He now returns every day, as a volunteer, to work with the school children.

In another case, a doorman at a big hotel in New York on retiring said, "I loved my job. I opened doors for presidents and kings. It's been a good life." A chewing gum factory worker, laid off after years of work said, "It's a beautiful place to work . . . just like home." These people view work not as an inalienable right but as a privilege.

Attitudes are related to beliefs and expectations. Unrealistic expectations lead to disappointment in ourselves or others. Even people we view as having glamorous, exciting careers dislike some parts of their work. Realistic expectations lead to more job satisfaction.

Attitudes are intricately bound to our personalities and perceptions of the world; thus it takes effort for us to change negative attitudes. However, William James said,

> The greatest discovery of our generation is that human beings by changing the inner attitudes of their minds can change the outer aspects of their lives.

One of the greatest gifts in life is to find work we love to do and then, incidentally, to make a living doing it.

## The Future of Work

General Motors, Chrysler, and Ford installed robots on their assembly lines. Robots have increased productivity and reduced the number of workers. Although evidence indicates automation will create some jobs *for skilled technicians*, many Americans fear being replaced by machines.

Government and industry have begun retraining programs for displaced workers. Although more computer programmers and electronic specialists are needed, fewer of these jobs require college degrees. World population will double in the next 35 years and will intensify the demand for housing and energy, thus creating new jobs. But there is concern that more and more people will be untrained for the complicated work of the future.

A second industrial revolution is under way. Many workers made idle by these changes must be retrained. Many of the jobs being lost will never return. Technological changes will make millions of people unemployable. Machines will relieve humans of dirty, dangerous, strenuous, menial, and repetitive tasks. In the factories of the future, the human workers will be engaged in installing, programming, monitoring, and repairing the robots that do all the direct labor.

Offices of the future will be automated with word processors and information systems that will eliminate such drudgery as filing and stenography. Many blue-collar jobs will be upgraded. Most people will have to switch careers at least once with constant retraining and reeducation a part of life.

With mandatory retirement outlawed, many older workers will want to continue working, possibly causing conflicts between young and old for jobs. Flexibility in retirement options includes incentives for retiring as early as age 55. Those who want to continue to work will find other opportunities. A person's working life will include two or three different jobs or professions.

Changes are often experienced as crises. For some, switching jobs is drastic, so they will choose the safety, routine, and security of the known. For others, however, switching jobs is exciting, so they will hop from job to job for the sake of change. Change brings stress—a tension of fear, loss of security, a need to maintain the status quo at the expense of excitement, risk, adventure, exploration, and self-actualization.

Some people invite change, are willing to explore new

possibilities, and want stimulation and change in work as part of the adventure of being alive. Intimate self-knowledge tells us when we have been in one job too long and whether the change is worth the risk.

Work gives us a community of other people in our lives. It provides us with a source of respect and self-esteem and, ultimately, with an opportunity for self-actualization—the potential for becoming all that we have the capacity to be and for making a difference in the world.

When we move toward a desired achievement, work is goal-directed behavior. Through work, we can order and define our life. Work gives us a sense of self. We earn recognition through a sense of competence in what we do. We also experience power, control, and self-respect through work.

For those persons who like control, a sense of forcing work into shape and creating order out of disorder is satisfying. The conquest of time through productivity, the feeling of achieving something or amounting to something comes through work.

Sometimes we also get public recognition for our services. Recognition answers the question, "How am I doing?" Internal rewards for work are experienced by our thinking, "I feel good about what I have done." Self-punishment is experienced by our thinking, "I feel bad about my work," "I did a lousy job," or "I have failed."

Some persons are motivated by working smart, accomplishing more in less time. Efficiency creates a sense of success by doing a lot in a little time. A job well done can be one of our most satisfying achievements. When balanced, the ambivalence between security and power results in harmony. Skating back and forth between opposing needs becomes increasingly important.

## Work and Leisure

Although most of us enjoy order and control over our environment, we tell ourselves, since we have worked hard all day, we can't be expected to work around the house at night or on the weekend. These hours we want to devote to leisure activities. The average adult has 45 hours a week of leisure time. In a recent leisure time survey, adults reported they spent

- 14 hours watching television
- 13 hours socializing—seeing friends, eating out, and so on

- 5 hours in sports activities
- 4 hours reading, including the newspaper
- 3 hours talking at home with family members
- 6 hours in various other activities

Eric Sevareid, news commentator, suggests the rise of leisure is a "dangerous threat to American society" because those who have the most leisure are the least equipped to make use of it. Those who are unskilled or uneducated, unable or unwilling to work, have 100 percent of their time free, making free time a burden. One out of ten persons today does not work. Researchers indicate a direct relationship between unstructured time and the crime rate among youthful offenders.

Hobbies play a role in filling leisure time, yet they are often utilitarian in nature. The do-it-yourself movement is a voluntary form of working. It also provides a worker with an excuse for seclusion and privacy. But if we designate hobbies as work, we resent having to do them. Ironically, what one person considers work another person considers leisure. Many find pleasure in doing what others dislike to do.

With time-saving equipment, shorter work weeks, and more vacation time, most Americans find themselves thinking about what they will do when they get off work. When confronted with the problem of deciding what to do with free time, the responsibility of free choice becomes a burden. Rather than think about (work at) how to spend leisure time, many people simply turn on the television.

Nonwork time includes personal care such as washing, dressing, eating, sleeping, and caring for the family and house. These are *not* considered either leisure time or free time activities. Since they must be done, most people say they are not enjoyable.

Some people, in deciding how they want to spend their free time, develop elaborate schedules. Sometimes the planning is more enjoyable than the activities. Elaborate vacation schedules covering as much territory as possible are attempts to use leisure time efficiently. Busy vacations include hectic travel schedules at one extreme or relaxing on the beach at the other extreme. People who know themselves well can best decide which leisure activities are suited to them.

Today, when asked whether they would prefer a raise in pay or more time off from work, many people opt for the latter. Still, the Department of Commerce reports only 58 out of every 100 people say they get "a great deal" of satisfaction with how they spend their leisure time.

Leisure time often involves spending money. Technology has made a bargain with us: "I will give you free time if you will promise to absorb my output." We do *not* spend money during working hours; we make it. As soon as we get off work, we become consumers, and consuming, in the form of spending money, takes time. Thus we busily go places, buy equipment, and invest in gadgets that overload our houses, closets, and garages. Then we have periodic garage sales to clear out the paraphernalia that seemed so attractive and indispensable when advertised. Advertisers have learned our patterns of consumption and appeal to our confusion about leisure.

Leisure is what we do when no one is telling us what to do. Often it feels like killing time or trying hard to have fun. After we spend our free time, we often feel we have wasted time. However, when we are wholly absorbed in either work or play, we are usually unaware of the passage of time.

Life can be divided into three stages: education in the first years of life, work in the middle years, and retirement in the last years. This arrangement puts us in three "boxes"—learning, achievement, and leisure. We can blend all these stages rather than keep them separated.

Many of us want to use our leisure time more effectively. The word *effective* doesn't seem appropriate to describe leisure. The words *enjoy, fun, relax, play* are the ones we use to describe what we think leisure should be. We believe work requires energy and drive, that it has a mission or meaning. Work tends to have a goal or purpose, a plan, intention, or design, whereas leisure is supposed to be spontaneous, without a goal or purpose. Leisure is supposed to be inseparable from entertainment, amusement, and distraction. If these rigid definitions create problems, we can redefine our terms.

Work is the way we tend the world, a way we connect with each other, a vigorous and vivid sign of life. Carlyle said, "All work . . . is noble." Leisure can be defined similarly.

Leisure, like work, *does* have a purpose. It can be a time of self-renewal, re-creation, rebuilding energies and talents and capabilities. Instead of thinking about leisure for the sake of leisure, we can, for example, regard free time as time to spend in the community—a time to learn something new or contribute what we know, a time to put back into society what we have taken out.

Composer John Ruskin said,

> There is no music in a rest but there's the making of music in it. And people are always missing that part of the life melody.

Like a symphony, we can blend education, work, and leisure rather than live them as separated stages in the life cycle. Life-long learning, lifelong working, and lifelong leisure begin in the early years, continue in the middle years, and end only at death. Leisure, rather than disengagement from life, can be a time to work, study, play, *and* enjoy life.

A crisis in intimacy often occurs at turning points in work. Work gives us opportunities for finding out who we are becoming and what we can potentially accomplish in life. Work also gives us opportunities to make connections with other people and to make contributions to our world. *Work is a form of love made invisible.*

# Intimacy and Paradox 10

> There is an astonishing contrast between the
> heavy perplexity that inhibits before the adven-
> ture has begun and the excitement that grips us
> the moment it begins. . . . As soon as a man
> makes up his mind to take the plunge into
> adventure, he is aware of a new strength he did
> not think he had, which rescues him from all
> his perplexities.
>
> Paul Tourier

America is changing. Demographic shifts indicate by 1990 Americans will be older, better educated, and more affluent. There will be fewer persons per household, fewer children, more working women, and more single-person households.

Napoleon said, "One must change one's tactics every ten years if one wishes to maintain one's superiority." With today's accelerating rate of change in attitudes, expectations, and values, ten years as a time frame would make us obsolete.

Along with cultural changes, the crisis in intimacy stems from internal, intrinsic contradictions that occur within each of us as we fight the battles between our public and private selves. What society wants from its citizens wars with what the family wants, and both conflict with what we want for ourselves as individuals. The sources of our ambivalence, both social and personal, are often hidden from us.

*Paradox occurs in the form of polar opposites, both simultaneously desirable or true.* These intrinsic contradictions occur throughout life. Paradox, when acknowledged, can be an invitation to self-knowledge and wisdom. In the very process of being human, polarity exists within us creating some of our strongest emotions and greatest challenges.

Historical and cultural forces tend to alienate us from ourselves and others. In the past, obligations to superiors provided strict dominant and submissive roles. With the discovery of the unique and separate individuality of each human being, family and cultural bonds have been weakened. We insist on personal liberation.

## Paradox in American Culture

Today, we benefit from great technological and scientific progress. We understand ourselves and our universe better than ever before. Paradoxically, we are not at ease in this world of our own making. We have become increasingly troubled about ourselves and our place in the world. We seem less certain of what is right or wrong, less sure that any meaning or purpose in the universe exists.

We praise and reward a person who is socially responsible at the same time that we are concerned about the pressures to conform. We admire independence, but suspect individual conscience may simply be the product of social conditioning. We have difficulty dealing with "personal values," a term that is at best ambiguous and that wars with words like *morality* and *ethics*. Thus we often find ourselves without direction, without something we can firmly commit to. No path seems to be laid out for us. Ultimately, in the confusion that engulfs us, we are driven to look inward for guidance.

Americans have the highest standard of living in the world even though millions of us live in poverty and deprivation. Thousands of jobs go unfilled while thousands of people cannot find employment. Our nation is founded on the ideals of liberty, equality, and opportunity, yet we find social unrest and personal disillusionment.

---

As a society, we send these kinds of double messages.

- We want our children to excel at the same time we want them to be obedient.
- We want our children to be achievers, to be creative, to be innovative at the same time we want them to conform.
- We want our children to be independent in mind and spirit, to think for themselves at the same time we want them to be popular and well liked.
- We want the warmth, love, and connection of having children

at the same time we do not want to tolerate wiggling, jumping, experimenting, hollering, or noise.
- We want to give our children freedom, responsibility, and self-control at the same time we want to control their behavior so it won't interfere with social needs.
- We want our children to be mentally alert, curious, and intellectually excited at the same time we want them to be quiet, unquestioning, and invisible when possible.

---

Considering these mixed messages, it is understandable—since we are products of our culture—that most of us experience conflict and ambivalence. We pass this confusion from one generation to another and will probably continue to do so.

Americans are criticized for overindulging their children at the same time they are accused of disliking them; children are overdependent on parents at the same time they are rebellious of parental authority. The ambivalence of love and resentment surrounds us.

We Americans believe our government is stupid, dishonest, and inefficient at the same time we think it is the best government in the world; in fact, we believe every other country ought to follow our example. Generally, we are a dissatisfied, restless, searching breed given to criticism. Yet 80 percent of Americans report they are "very proud" of their nationality. We believe in the American Dream and the American Way of Life.

In a recent survey, 64 percent of the public said they were "willing to sacrifice" to get the economy back on track. Yet 53 percent said no to cuts in health and education; 57 percent said no to cuts in spending on the poor; 69 percent said no to higher taxes; and 81 percent said no to higher levels of unemployment. They also said no to higher levels of air and water pollution, higher prices, and cuts in social security.

Americans feel pessimistic about uneducated, untrained, unemployed nonworkers. The young are unhappy about having to pay high social security taxes to support the old. Parents feel disillusioned about children who cannot read or write. And taxpayers are distressed about poverty and crime. Still, most Americans are generally optimistic about the future and have high hopes and personal aspirations.

Reason alone cannot bring us understanding. Although we acknowledge the power and influence of scientific thinking, we have lost confidence in the scientific method to answer questions about meaning and purpose in life. The first attitude glorifies rational thought, and the second belittles it. These paradoxes live together in the same house of our minds.

Every generalization we make can be canceled by another. This world we live in appears as a phenomenal duality. An impersonal, objective world outside us envelops our personal, subjective world. *Life is ambiguity.* We function and move through life without absolutes and deprived of certainties, continually making new judgments and decisions without answers or knowing how our decisions will work out. *Paradox is at the very core of being human.*

### The Cost of Intimacy

The freely choosing, responsible, "personal self" yearns for liberation. Self-intimacy initially is gained by concentrating on the self at the cost of shutting out the family and smaller community. Through self-love, rather than approval from others, we find the courage and strength to be authentically ourselves. While we attempt to separate ourselves from the family and smaller communities, corporations and government bureaucracies along with mass communication spin webs around us. The "public self" belongs to legal, social, technical, and public groups. In this process, the public self—part of mass-market industrialism—becomes detached from the personal self.

The crisis in intimacy stems partly from loss of self in public roles. We struggle to free ourselves from the restrictions of family, community, and public bonds. Intimacy presumes the suspension of the public self. As we cut ourselves loose, we long for attachments. Based on tolerance, trust, and deep affection, we rely on the support of family, friends, and intimates for the suspension of these public identities.

In consideration for those we love, we try, at times, to suspend our self-centeredness. But enforced intimacy in the family results in our developing defenses against the invasion of the autonomous self. Often, youthful friendships are based on a common hostility to parents and siblings. We want a sense of attachment, a sense of community, a network of people, yet these attachments cost us our personal freedom.

We constantly find ourselves waring between wanting close, intimate relationships and wanting freedom from interpersonal squabbles. Two University of Washington sociologists, Phillip Blumstein and Pepper Schwartz, interviewed 6,000 couples and compiled 656 pages of information. The primary interpersonal conflicts center on sex, work, and money.

In *American Couples*, the researchers analyze financial aspects of intimate relationships. Money is often a more taboo topic than sex. Traditionally, married couples pooled their resources, but today fewer women than men want to pool funds. Having control over personal finances is one way we measure power. Having separate money creates independence. And having no financial entanglements makes it easier to end a relationship.

Blumstein and Schwartz found that 59 percent of wives but only 39 percent of husbands are "relationship-centered." Each person chooses between work and the relationship. Most of the couples interviewed have at least one relationship-centered partner, or the relationship ends. Conflicts over sex, work, and money usually revolve around issues of power and control, which war with intimacy.

To avoid these power struggles, some people live alone. Contrary to popular belief, many "loners" live alone by choice. To maintain control of their social worlds, loners, like monks and forest rangers, maintain active mental lives—reading, studying, working. People who live alone are no more likely to say they are lonely than people who live with others. Some people learn to appreciate solitude as an antidote to social overload. Loners want control of their lives. One widow says,

> I can't tell you how wonderful it is to be alone. I feel calm and at peace. Because I am not searching for a mate, I look at people in an entirely different way. People I might not otherwise be attracted to become interesting, enjoyable, and amusing. When I do go out, anything that happens can be enjoyed because I no longer have preconceived notions about what "ought" to happen. It's a freedom I never could have imagined.

Executives and managers of organizations, who are said to hold "the loneliest job in the world," report they are less lonely than any other occupational group. The relative isolation "at the top" depends on our vantage point.

Although old saws like, "Money can't buy happiness" may have a grain of truth in them, a direct correlation seems to exist between loneliness and income. The higher the income, the less people say they experience loneliness.

Loneliness scores correlate with measures of low self-esteem. Younger people consistently experience more loneliness than older people. Women say they are more lonely than men. Poor people say they are more lonely than affluent people. Most of us steadily search for a better balance between personal autonomy and interpersonal intimacy.

As our knowledge increases, our understanding seems to decrease. The confidence and capacity of a person to understand the self and personal life seems to be undermined as our world becomes more complex. The human ability to reason no longer seems to ensure understanding. Perhaps freedom of thought is a delusion. Unless we can become aware of the various sources that direct our thoughts, we are prisoners of past conditioning and habits.

How capable are we as individuals to uncover the unconscious beliefs, desires, feelings, and thoughts that influence us? Our efforts to understand ourselves and our world are at once helped and hindered by the time and place in which we are born—the views, traditions, and characteristics of our culture.

Our language, which affects our beliefs, attitudes, and values, is like a prison inside a prison. Thus it is paradoxical that science, which strives to gain knowledge through thought alone, is also a prisoner of language. Once we have defined and labeled a problem, we have, in effect, created a problem.

*Divine discontent* is an intimate part of being human, so we skate back and forth between our public and private selves, between interpersonal intimacy and personal autonomy, seldom suspended in a restful balance for long. We can, however, learn to live in a confusing world and tolerate being pulled by opposing forces, when we recognize paradox is part of the human condition.

### Opposing Forces

Opposing forces in our private lives stem from the need to know the self and the fear of knowing; from wanting to be close to others and wanting to be free; from being afraid of change and inviting change; from the drive for safety and security and the drive for stimulation and adventure; from wanting to be the "ideal" self in an ideal world and being forced to live with the "real" self in a real world. Each of us lives with conflicts between love and achievement, attachment and independence, compliance and self-esteem, social good and individual well being.

Freedom comes with self-trust, from commitment to self-knowledge and self-completion, and from the willingness to acknowledge paradox, tension, and conflict as essential to life. No strategy designed to keep us safe can always entirely forestall trouble. The insistence on safety reminds us of the possibilities of danger. The self-starting, self-rewarding, self-propelling person finds moments of genuine inner fulfillment with the development of personal abilities. This kind of *intrapersonal* intimacy grows over time accompanied by the willingness to be insecure.

Our goal is to live as effectively as possible. Failure and frustration are prerequisites of life, and dissatisfaction often precedes change. Personal progress entails risk, frustration, and discomfort. Self-esteem and self-realization come with the creative drive to attain worthwhile objectives through autonomous decisions accompanied by the willingness to take responsibility for those decisions even when they do not work.

We contribute to mutual faith in humankind when we share the strength and courage to stand alone and choose for ourselves. Self-love enables us to build loving relationships with others, which increases the well of human support and empathy.

### The Cost of Autonomy

Ezra Pound said, "A slave is one who waits for someone else to free him!" The cause of slavery lies within the person enslaved. We can choose for ourselves or have others choose for us. The person who lives most of life allowing others to choose for him or her often feels bitter and resentful. Lacking autonomy, these people feel they are at the mercy of others and therefore not responsible for their lives.

*Autonomy means self-rule.* Choosing autonomy as a personal goal can lead to satisfaction. The autonomous person knows what he or she wants and makes valid choices to reach these goals. Through developing autonomy, we escape some of the tangle of confusions and contradictions we find in society.

The autonomous person through self-knowledge sets goals. Goals give us clarity and direction. We find fulfillment and security as we gain competence in personal growth. The autonomous person recognizes time is life and chooses to make the most of both. One woman said,

I know that I am going to die and I accept that fact. I want to live fully in the here and now. My living today is enriched by my knowledge, exploration, and understanding of my past—both personal and cultural. I love my past, including the painful parts from which I learned so much. I have absolutely no regrets or resentments. Although many of my past choices did not work out, I feel no guilt. I have many goals for my future and hope to live a long life.

Living encompasses a past–present–future continuity. Regret over past decisions, bitterness about past experiences, resentment at past betrayals—all these are expressions of incompetence through overconcern with someone else's approval or an unwillingness to accept responsibility for one's own choices. The expression, "If only I had . . . " implies regret. Understanding paradox lets us set goals and enjoy moving toward them.

---

To discover what you want in life, answer these questions.

- If I were to die tonight, what would I have missed that would make me feel sad?
- What would I like to do with the rest of my life?
- What interest would I like to pursue?
- What have I not seen or done that I would like to?

---

To a degree, we are more or less in charge of our lives, or we are controlled by internal or external forces that we submit to. At any time, we can choose to review our lives and change our attitudes toward our environment. Self-acceptance promotes strength, confidence, and the courage to pursue goals. However, we can conform when conforming is functional rather than rebel merely for the sake of rebellion. We can choose social beliefs and actions when they fit our own interests. Often social interests and personal interests coincide.

*Autonomy is the capacity to make valid choices about our own behavior based on personal decisions.* To the extent that we make choices based on external coercion or internal rebellion, we are incapable of autonomy. For most of us, internal limitations, those we impose on ourselves, outweigh external ones.

Our society values autonomy. When autonomy is not disruptive, we encourage it in our children. But in a conflict between an adult and a child, the adult usually has power over the child's behavior. However, adults have little control over a child's perceptions and attitudes. We do not control their minds.

Controlling antisocial behavior and simultaneously encouraging self-acceptance is possible by offering a child opportunities to make choices and to take responsibility for those choices, both the ones that work and the ones that don't. Supporting and encouraging a child's autonomy and individuality is one source of enjoyment in life.

No one is totally autonomous. Autonomy is one end of a continuum with adjustment and conformity at the other end. Autonomy is choosing a direction in which to move.

Personal needs for material abundance, housing, food, and medical care are all technologically within our grasp today. The real struggle lies inside each of us. We must resolve our private conflicts internally instead of acting them out in antisocial ways. We are bound together primarily by choice—by wanting to give and receive warmth and association.

Traditionally, we assume there is an inevitable conflict between the individual and society. But when we look closely, personal and social satisfactions are often allied. Increased autonomy leads to social concern. Autonomous persons can choose to act in socially constructive ways, for the ultimate goal is to *celebrate the self in a social context.*

## Choosing a Philosophical View

The philosopher Nietzsche said, "Man always acts rightly." One student interprets Nietzsche this way:

> Given the situation I am in at this time in my life and given all the information I have and given the person I am at this moment, I am making the best of all possible choices that I know how to make for myself.

Jean Paul Sartre says we live in precisely that state we choose to be in. If we believed we would be better off in some other state, we would be there.

We are where we are because we have chosen the priorities of our lives, even when we try to deny the negative aspects of our decisions. As there is no sun that doesn't have a shadow, so there is no choice that doesn't have both negative and positive aspects. Denying the negative aspects of our choices is unauthentic and causes internal disunity.

Ralph Waldo Emerson wrote two short poems and one long essay on the subject of compensation. In our Western culture, we have a great deal of difficulty understanding the dualism that underlies the condition of human existence. Emerson says,

> Every sweet hath its sour; every evil its good. . . . For everything you have missed, you have gained something else; and for everything you gain, you lose something.

For every choice we make, there are both advantages and disadvantages—a college education, marriage, children, home ownership—every dream has drawbacks when transposed into reality. A good life costs, and denying the price is self-deception.

Philosophers have debated since time began whether humans are primarily good or evil, altruistic or selfish, cooperative or competitive, gregarious or self-centered. On these issues, we do not have to take a position. Denial of reality, of any disagreeable or unpleasant information about ourselves, in the form of defense mechanisms and self-deception can be discarded. Human beings are neither intrinsically good nor bad but human and responsible.

Another great debate centers on the issue of free will versus determinism. The behaviorists search for the roots of human problems in biology and genetics. Those who do not want to take responsibility for their lives claim that, given our society as well as other outside forces, humans have scant control over their own lives. In contrast, the humanistic existentialists tell us we have free choice for which we are responsible; human existence precedes essence; and with every choice we make, we create the essence of who we are.

Norman Cousins, a writer, explained his position in a little essay, "A Game of Cards," in which he wrote, "The hand that is dealt you represents determinism. The way you play your hand represents free will."

A man in midlife said,

> I cannot be a woman. I was born a man. I did not choose my genes or my parents or the historical period in which I was born. But I am willing to take responsibility for *all* the choices I have made in my life. For everything I have done, I reaped a harvest and paid a price. Given the person I was at any particular time, with whatever information I had, I made choices for which I am responsible.

This man's statement is not a matter of "truth". It's a belief that we have *some* choice about how we want to perceive ourselves and our lives. Perceptions of reality are not matters for debate and are unrelated to the concept of truth.

We create our perceptions of the world according to our personal needs, motives, and interests. We screen what we receive and organize our experiences to see what we want to see. Each of us makes up our personal world through selecting what will fit with our past experiences, values, and goals.

Truth cannot be arrived at through perceptions because no two people perceive, hear, see, think, or feel things the same way. We have preconceived mental sets, and we fit new information into these preset patterns. Thus our choices are intimately connected to how we interpret our ambiguous pasts.

This process of organizing sensory stimulation into patterns is highly selective and affects our experiences of other people. It is the foundation for our concepts of intimacy. We categorize and classify people into sets according to size and shape; then we create some stability about them. Our original impressions of them become fixed, as theirs of us become fixed.

Some structure and stability are needed. We cannot deal with a world where every experience, every new person, is a new beginning. The confusion would be like that of the newborn baby. The world, ourselves, and other people must be ordered into some kind of meaningful, manageable experience. Thus past experiences play a necessary role in our perceptions and how we create personal reality.

### Intimacy and Conflicting Realities

*Our freedom to choose makes us responsible for our values.* No predetermined human nature exists that defines us or gives us a value system. We must all come to some conclusions about what we want to make of our lives and our relationships. At the same time, we must deal with what is real for others. When we deny other people's reality, we cannot relate to them. Reality is split. We create our own reality and must allow others to create theirs.

One of our basic struggles is the conflict between our own view of ourselves (our subjective perceptions) and the intrusion of others' perceptions, which threatens our subjectivity. If we live through the perceptions of others, we forsake freedom and choice. Without the perceptions of others, however, we cannot discover who we are. We need each other as mirrors to reflect back what we see without living the images created by others.

Relationships are based on equality and respect for others in the context of holding onto one's own perceptions. We are free to be all we are, to pay attention, to take our relationships seriously, and to respond honestly to one another.

*A relationship is a challenge of two realities confronting each other.* No one can say suffering the pain and joy of an intense relationship is better than suffering loneliness or a tranquil, safe, unemotional life. Confrontation involves a direct challenge from one person to another. Some people thrive on confrontation, and some people choose not to confront.

An independent view of the world without interpersonal commitments has its positive aspects. To attempt deep relationships is, at times, risky, unsafe, and unpredictable. One goal we can trust is to respond authentically to one another. We are always subject to chance. We cannot know what will happen in the next second; we simply make reasonable guesses.

What happens tomorrow, next week, or next month is still less certain. And what we think about next year is pure imagination. Yet we can live each day, barring great accidents, choosing our own attitudes toward our lives.

The total situation is less important than the attitudes we choose to take about ourselves and our relationships. We can function without being able to control all the variables. The self transcends chance by reacting freely to the unexpected in relationships.

The crisis in intimacy comes out of the human relationships game, where the rules are eternally changing but never made clear. It is a game we withdraw from only at death. Most of the time, we are just playing in the mud of conflicting opinions, beliefs, and assumptions.

We are all born into this complex cultural system that structures what we see, how we talk, and what we can talk about. It gives us a language and a set of rules to play by. The script was written before we were born. It includes all the objects and events that already had names and meanings before we arrived. It also includes all the values and ethical standards, all the laws and systems that we learn without knowing what they are or how they will affect us. Many of these standards contradict one another. Exploring and questioning our cultural heritage are part of finding out how we got to this place in historical time.

### Intimacy and Freedom

The philosopher Santayana said,

> Absolute liberty . . . is impracticable; it is a foolish challenge thrown by a newborn insect buzzing against the universe; it is incompatible with more than one pulse of life. All the declarations of independence in the world will not render anybody really independent.

Freedom has many definitions and can be applied in many situations. Our first freedom is physical; we are free to move about and cannot be locked in a dungeon at someone's behest. Beyond that, we want the freedom to provide ourselves, through our own efforts, adequate food, housing, and clothing.

Since we are feeling and thinking human beings, our next level of freedom is to use our energies for productive enterprises of our own choice in work and in recreation, to use our minds productively. The limits to freedom of thought are fashioned in our childhood by the attitudes and values of our parents and siblings. What we feel, think, and believe begin to be formed in the family.

Without the transmittal of values, there would be no civilization, culture, or history. These values in life come through family relationships. The long dependency in our first years of life leaves us with an ineradicable hunger for contact, response, love and warmth, the give and take of human responsiveness. The paradox is we learn *through* dependency. As children we need love, approval, and protection. And these needs socialize us.

When we finally become socialized, we become an active part of society, which puts further limitations on our freedom while providing us with other advantages like education and productive work. We must rebel against society. Thoreau went into the woods, and Gauguin to Tahiti. Some people become revolutionaries; others, criminals.

Every society necessarily acts like a parent restricting its children. At the same time, society is a fellowship, a sharing of vital interests with restrictions. The unconscious identity among members of a society is the cement that holds it together. Our common assumptions and compatible goals serve as a buffer against isolation.

One paradox of freedom is, in seeking it, we become our own jailers. By breaking tie after tie until we are unconnected, we may end up in a solitary confinement of our own making. A pervasive ambivalence keeps some of us, at certain times in our lives, from making decisions or commitments. A decision or commitment positions us in society and locks us into something. Today, there seems to be a solidarity of uncommitted people confirming one another's lack of commitment.

The crisis in intimacy can come from a striving for the mirage of absolute freedom or from an insatiable longing for community. Although we may not choose to live indefinitely in isolation, we find only a partial satisfaction in a series of interlocking relationships—with the self, family, friends, professional associates, society, and finally, humanity itself.

One goal is to create for ourselves a balance between personal and social freedoms to achieve a kind of harmony. Through faith in being human, a balanced responsibility for self and others, and at times, a commitment to involvement in the world, we can find, each day, satisfaction in our lives.

## Choosing a World View

Each of us is free to choose an attitude and a view of the world. Our perceptions of our world are created by us, and we are responsible for them. It's much easier to sit and watch accidents or injustices than to work for change. In a crisis, it takes courage to seek some degree of correction.

We have some serious problems to solve in this century. In view of these problems, some people have become pessimistic and cynical. They have lost faith in government, church, and human beings generally. Although premature, these people predict global thermal pollution, overpopulation, starvation, widespread crime, economic disaster, and nuclear war. Despair is not only unpleasant and unproductive, it can also be contagious. People practice feeling helpless until they feel comfortable with despair. Then they want company.

Other ages have been far worse than ours. The Roman era was a time of extraordinary cruelty. The Elizabethan period was full of diseases, ignorance, and incredible poverty. Cynical people measure in only one direction—from how things are to how they think things ought to be.

Maintaining a negative stance in life requires some distortion. Pessimists must not notice good, and kind or thoughtful acts must be ignored. They exploit their bad feelings by selecting and blowing-up ugly incidents and experiences. They dwell on painful relationships or destructive public scenes.

Problem solving takes thought, work, energy, and concern. Neither will power nor knowledge nor ethical concern alone will solve problems. But with imagination and commitment, we can find solutions to small parts of large social problems.

We can assert our birthright as free persons to choose not only if and when but also where and how we will get involved: pollution, highway safety, consumer protection, civil rights. We can volunteer to work on social problems such as drugs, alcohol, child abuse, and suicide. By becoming aware of problems and calling attention to them, we can commit ourselves to human survival—personal and social.

Even with mass media's obsession with what is wrong, even with public communication centered on crisis, and even if we find a general loss of faith around us, we can choose to find examples of positive social change, of people working to help others, of compassion and kindness, of sacrifice and sharing.

## Dangerous Opportunity

The crisis in intimacy presents us with opportunities in disguise. We can reexamine our expectations to see if they are unrealistic. We can examine and question basic cultural beliefs, such as humans should be loving, caring, kind, thoughtful, considerate of others, and unselfish; we are never all these things all the time. We can notice that when we change our attitudes, we change the outer aspects of our lives. For example, we can view struggle, tension, and confusion as emotions that lead us forward and motivate us to find answers, conquer mountains, explore new territories, and fly into the unknown.

Fear of failure or of making mistakes takes on a different cloak when we acknowledge painful experiences contribute to self-wisdom, and compassion for others makes us more valuable as human beings. As a result, we can move beyond the passionate expression of self-interest and choose to live interdependently. Failure to achieve absolute justice need not make us obsessed with what is negative. We can reject cynicism and despair for a brighter, nobler view of our potential—not as a reality but as a goal, as a vision to pursue and work toward. We can hope that others will join us in our common cause. The issues of human survival belong to us all.

Each of us has interests and values that conflict with the interests and values of others. Sometimes that is painful, but a world where all of us had the same interests and values would be insufferable. Conflicts within the individual, the family, business and government, and between nations cause discomfort. However, we can also appreciate tension between opposites as creative contradiction, as an opportunity for growth and change.

Whatever may divide us—whether culture, ethnicity, world view, ideology, religion, or generation—we are all united in a common fate, the issue of human survival. And in this respect, not one of us can escape the necessity of choice. Each of us can choose, in some small way, the role of trustee for a small planet.

# Bibliography

Audrey, Robert. *The Territorial Imperative*. Dell, New York, 1966.

Bernard, Jessie. *The Future of Marriage*. Yale University Press, New Haven, Conn., 1982.

Berne, Eric. *Games People Play*. Grove Press, New York, 1964.

Bolles, Richard N. *The Three Boxes of Life: And How to Get out of Them*. Ten Speed Press, Berkeley, Calif., 1978.

Brown, Barbara B. *Supermind: The Ultimate Energy*. Harper & Row, New York, 1980.

Buscaglia, Leo. *Love*. Charles B. Slack, Thorofare, N.J., 1979.

Carr, Jacquelyn B. *Communicating and Relating*. Wm. C. Brown, Dubuque, Iowa, 1984.

———. *Communicating with Myself: A Journal*. Wm. C. Brown, Dubuque, Iowa, 1984.

———. *Equal Partners: The Art of Creative Marriage*. R & E Publishers, Saratoga, Calif., 1987.

Erickson, Erick. *Identity: Youth and Crisis*. W.W. Norton, New York, 1968.

Freud, Sigmund. *An Outline of Psychoanalysis*. W.W. Norton, New York, 1949.

Fromm, Erich. *The Art of Loving*. Harper & Row, New York, 1956.

———. *Escape from Freedom*. Holt, Rinehart & Winston, New York, 1963.

Fromme, Allan. *The Ability to Love*. Farrar, Straus & Giroux, New York, 1963.

Gardner, John W. *Self-Renewal*. Harper & Row, New York, 1963.

Gibb, Jack R. "Defensive Communication." *The Journal of Communication*, 11(3), Sept., 1961.

Green, Hannah. *I Never Promised You a Rose Garden*. Signet Books, New York, 1964.

Greene, L. *Relating*. Samuel Weiser, New York, 1977.

Hall, Edward. T. *Beyond Culture*. Anchor/Doubleday, New York, 1976.

———. *The Silent Language*. Fawcett, Greenwich, Conn., 1961.

Harris, Thomas A. *I'm O.K., You're O.K.* Harper & Row, New York, 1967.

Hoffer, Eric. *The Ordeal of Change*. Harper & Row, New York, 1952.

Huxley, Laura Archera. *You Are Not the Target*. Farrar, Straus & Giroux, New York, 1963.

James, William. *The Varieties of Religious Experience*. New American Library, New York, 1958.

Jourard, Sidney M. *The Transparent Self*. Van Nostrand, New York, 1962.

Jung, C.G. *The Undiscovered Self*. Mentor Books, New York, 1957.

———. *Man and His Symbols*. Dell, New York, 1968.

Koestenbaum, Peter. *Managing Anxiety: The Power of Knowing Who You Are*. Prentice-Hall, Englewood Cliffs, N.J., 1974.

Lakein, Alan. *How to Get Control of Your Time and Your Life*. Peter H. Wyden, New York, 1973.

Leakey, Richard E. *Origins*. E.P. Dutton, New York, 1977.

Leonard, George. *Transformation*. Dell, New York, 1972.

Lindgren, Henry Clay. *How to Live with Yourself and Like It*. Faucett, New York, 1963.

Lorenz, Konrad. *On Human Aggression*. Harcourt Brace & World, New York, 1966.

Maslow, Abraham H. *Motivation and Personality*. Harper & Row, New York, 1954.

———. *Toward a Psychology of Being*. Van Nostrand, New York, 1962.

May, Rollo. *Love and Will*. W.W. Norton, New York, 1969.

Mayeroff, Milton. *On Caring*. Perennial Library, New York, 1971.

Menninger, Karl. *Man Against Himself*. Harcourt Brace & World, New York, 1938.

Metzner, Ralph. *Know Your Type: Maps of Identity*. Anchor/ Doubleday, New York, 1979.

Montague, Ashley. *Touching: The Human Significance of the Skin*. Harper & Row, New York, 1971.

———. *The Nature of Human Aggression*. Oxford Press, New York, 1976.

Morgan, George W. *The Human Predicament: Dissolution and Wholeness*. Dell, New York, 1968.

Morris, Desmond. *Intimate Behavior*. Bantam Books, New York, 1971.

Moustakas, Clark E. *Loneliness*. Prentice-Hall, Englewood Cliffs, N.J., 1961.

Murphy, Gardner. *Outgrowing Self-Deception*. Basic Books, New York, 1975.

O'Neill, Nena, and O'Neill, George. *Shifting Gears: Finding Security in a Changing World.* Avon Books, New York, 1975.

Otto, Herbert A., ed. *Love Today: A New Exploration.* Dell, New York, 1972.

Packard, Vance. *The Sexual Wilderness.* Simon & Schuster, New York, 1968.

Perls, Frederick S. *In and Out the Garbage Pail.* Real People Press, Moab, Utah, 1969.

Putney, Snell, and Putney, Gail J. *Normal Neurosis—The Adjusted American.* Harper & Row, New York, 1964.

Rand, Ayn. *The Virtue of Selfishness: A New Concept of Egoism.* Signet Books, New York, 1964.

Rogers, Carl. *On Becoming a Person.* Houghton Mifflin, Boston, 1961.

Rubin, Theodore Isaac. *Lisa and David.* Ballantine Books, New York, 1961.

Samples, Bob. *The Metaphoric Mind: A Celebration of Creative Consciousness.* Addison-Wesley, Reading, Mass., 1976.

Sapirstein, Milton R. *Paradoxes of Everyday Life.* Fawcett, New York, 1955.

Satir, Virginia. *People Making.* Science & Behavior Books, Palo Alto, Calif., 1972.

Seabury, David. *The Art of Selfishness.* Simon & Schuster, New York, 1937.

Seyle, Hans. *Stress Without Distress.* J.P. Lippincott, Philadelphia, 1974.

Shostrom, Everett L. *Man the Manipulator.* Bantam Books, New York, 1968.

Toffler, Alvin. *Future Shock.* Random House, New York, 1970.

———. *The Third Wave.* William Morrow, New York, 1980.

Veroff, Joseph, and Feld, Sheila. *Marriage & Work in America.* Van Nostrand Reinhold, New York, 1970.

Walster, E., and Walter, G. W. *A New Look at Love.* Addison-Wesley, Reading, Mass., 1978.

Wanderer, Zev, and Fabian, Erika. *Making Love Work: New Techniques in the Art of Staying Together.* G. Putnum & Son, New York, 1979.

Watts, Alan. *The Book: On the Taboo Against Knowing Who You Are.* Collier Books, New York, 1966.

Zilbergeld, Bernie. *Male Sexuality: A Guide to Sexual Fulfillment.* Little Brown, Boston, 1978.

# Index